REVIEWS OF *GAME-CHANGING ADVISORY BOARDS*

"Every business owner should read this book. I have served on several advisory boards with the authors. The processes they describe work. Their concept of Sustainable Value and the disciplines needed to deliver it are grounded in the real world of building strong companies."

Phil Matthews
Chairman of Zodiac Marine and Pool, a Carlyle company.
Former Chairman of Wolverine Worldwide and Bell Helmets

"This is the best book I have seen on advisory boards. *Game-Changing Advisory Boards* is packed with processes and lessons learned in the practice of private company governance. The Value Wheel concept should shape every board meeting agenda."

M. Christian Mitchell
President and Chairman of the Southern California Chapter
of the National Association of Corporate Directors

"This book should be in every CEO's library! We created our advisory board over 20 years ago and that decision generated one of the most powerful catalytic effects for the growth of our firm. The concepts in this book took us to another level."

Mike Kiley, CEO & Founder, Chamberlain Group

"Bill and John make the case for Advisory Boards. This is a must read for anyone serious about getting their business to the next level! A group of outsiders who can bring creativity, challenge, accountability and insights to a growing enterprise is invaluable."

Richard Carr, Former CEO and Vice Chairman of
Vistage International

W9-BUS-694

"This is a superb roadmap for private companies to get the benefits and rewards from outside trusted advisors. This book tells owners and leaders how to raise the bar and get the benefit of perspective, clarity and focus. Having been on both sides of many Boards, this is a must read."

Rick Flatow, Consultant, Advisor, Director & former CEO of public and private companies

"This book is a must read for every business owner who wants to take their business to new levels. The authors bring a lifetime of experience to a critical topic."

John Izzo, Ph.D. author of *Stepping Up* and *Awakening Corporate Soul*

"Congratulations on putting this great work together. It is an excellent resource for private business owners. It gives them the "how-to" along with the theory for effectively setting up and using an Advisory Board to help add value to their business. At Ontic, our advisory board helped transition business leadership from the owners to the new CEO, and create a clear objective to triple the value of the business. Three year later, we realized that value in the sale of the company."

Jim Gerwien, CEO, Extant Components Group

"Getting the right people for your board is key. By following the ideas provided by Bill and John, you will be able to fulfill your vision by selecting the best board members. With a strong board and a great team, you can hit it out of the park!

Dana Borowka, CEO, Lighthouse Consulting Services

"Game Changing is the right title! The tested board practices in this book change companies and the way they are managed. I have seen how they help owners, boards and their teams make better decisions and build long-term, sustainable value. This is excellent advice from two men who have played the game from the corner office and the board room."

Peter Alexander, CEO and Board member of BMC, Boise, ID

"Leveraging the wisdom of a small set of an experienced and trusted set of advisors can be the secret sauce that separates winners and losers in entrepreneurial pursuits. In *Game-Changing Advisory Boards*, Hawfield and Zaepfel have captured the essential ingredients of sustainable value creation. They provide strong evidence that a carefully selected advisory board that is strategic, connected, and knowledgeable can be the powerful inner circle that focuses the meanderings of an often too lonely entrepreneur. Should the owner listen to those sages that he or she now holds close, the venture can become a more fruitful and rewarding experience."

Alfred E. Osborne, Jr., Ph. D.
Senior Associate Dean and Professor of Global Economics
and Management
Faculty Director, Harold and Pauline Price Center for
Entrepreneurial Studies, UCLA Anderson School of
Management

"Game-Changing Advisory Boards offers a prescription for success to privately held entrepreneurial companies. Over the past two decades, a number of my Vistage members have also created a professional advisory board – the results have been synergistic and successful."

Pete Lakey
Master Chair, Vistage International, Advisory board
member

"I highly recommend this book to all owners and CEO's of privately held companies. I have personally served with Bill on four advisory boards and each one has contributed to extraordinary growth in sustainable value. Join a long list of successful companies."

Michael Laney, Board member and Executive Coach,
former Chairman of NACD, Portland, OR

"Owner-operators of mid-sized companies need real help in accessing outside expertise to continue to grow their businesses. Hawfield and Zaepfel have synthesized their rich and deep professional experience and translated it into a book that makes it very practical for their audience to succeed. This will work. The real challenge for the owner-operator is to not only buy this book and actually read it but to commit to doing the work to turn this from idea to everyday reality inside their business. If they do, the benefits will be not just for the business, but for the owner and her or his family as well."

Lawrence King, PhD., Vistage Speaker and Vistage Chair Emeritus

"Bill and John are the Masters! An effective board catalyzes an entirely higher level of strategic thinking, leadership, and aptitude development of the senior management team. Applying the ideas in this book will accelerate building your personal wealth and transferable value in your business."

Brian Stone, CEO, American Stone Partners, Board member

"A game-changing advisory board moved my business from merely successful to a highly dynamic, highly profitable, energetically relevant, middle market business. By establishing an advisory board, now a statutory board, and integrating some of the disciplines outlined in *Game-Changing Advisory Boards*, our company has experienced an upswing in function, efficiency and morale. Communication, strategic planning and operating goals are intentionally valued and discussed by trusted advisors, experienced CEOs, who have a broader perspective than I could ever have alone. I cannot thank John Zaepfel and Keith Swayne enough for their support, advisement and calm, steady push for best practices success!"

Ted Ballou, CEO, Mitchell Rubber Products, Inc.

"*Game-Changing Advisory Boards* offers a substantial competitive advantage. It shows you how to build your personal brain trust of outside advisors. In the information age, whoever has the most knowledge wins. Use these concepts to make your business a winner!"

Mark R. Edwards, PhD,
Professor, Strategic Entrepreneurship, Arizona State
University and co-author of the business best-seller
360° Feedback.

"*Game-Changing Advisory Boards,* not only spells out the why, but it educates, those willing, on how to do it right from selecting a board to getting the most out of your investment of time and $$. Doing it right can be the difference between failure and great success and as hard as it is for CEOs to ask for help, that might just be their defining moment."

Mark Filanc, Chairman and CEO, Filanc Construction

"John Zaepfel has provided tremendous insight to our company as a member of our Advisory Board for years. It is a fantastic that he and Bill Hawfield are now sharing their game-changing approach through this fascinating new book. I highly recommend it to any medium-size organization looking to develop sustainable, profitable business growth for the future."

Thomas Silber, President and CEO, BIVAR, Inc.

Game-Changing

Advisory Boards

Leveraging Outside Wisdom
To Deliver Sustainable Value

William Hawfield

John Zaepfel

THE BOARD GROUP
PUBLISHING COMPANY

Published by The Board Group Publishing Company
3075 E. Thousand Oaks Blvd.
Westlake Village, CA 91362

This publication is designed to provide authoritative information about the subject matter covered. It is sold with the understanding that the publisher and the authors are not rendering legal, accounting, or other professional services. If legal or financial assistance is required, the reader should seek the counsel of a competent professional.

For order information or special discounts for bulk purchases, please contact The Board Group at 805-497-3040 or by email at GameChanging@theboardgroup.com

Dedication

To the men and women

who are owners of privately-held companies.

You build and sustain organizations.

You consistently serve your customers' needs.

You create millions of meaningful jobs.

You take the personal risk.

You bear the stress of unrelenting challenges.

You are real heroes.

TABLE OF CONTENTS

PART III: LEVERAGING ADVISORS TO BUILD SUSTAINABLE VALUE

PART IV: COMPLETING YOUR END GAME

Preface

You built your business. Your company has succeeded despite constant challenges from competitive attacks, government involvement, market declines and rising costs. You take big risks every day to survive and build long-term value. The families of those who work with you, your customers and vendors all rely on your company's success.

What keeps you awake at night? Negative cash flow? People problems? Partners or family? Customer problems? An expensive opportunity? Selling or keeping your business?

If you make good decisions, create game-changing strategies and take timely actions, you could thrive and build sustainable value. If you make poor decisions, you could pay a hefty price or even lose everything.

What if you had a council of wise, successful, independent business people who know you and your business well and are fully committed to your success? Imagine how their wisdom could help you make consistently excellent decisions, manage execution, and leverage your strengths to succeed.

That wise council is available to you. It is a professional advisory board (PABoard). This book defines the professional advisory board process. The authors have used the process in nearly 90 companies with combined revenues of over $5 Billion. You will learn how to create a PABoard to attain the business and personal outcomes you want.

You will find the ideas and stories from owners of privately-held companies who used PABoards to prepare their companies for sale. Collectively, they received over $1.1 billion when they sold. You will also read about owners who are using PABoards today to professionalize their business and build greater sustainable value for future generations.

WHO SHOULD READ THIS BOOK?

This book speaks first to owners of privately-held companies who are ready to focus on building sustainable value for themselves and their employees. They are willing to make changes to professionalize the business game they are playing.

Board members, CEOs, and senior management will find processes and structures to help them govern their companies. If they use the models, the checklists, and the underlying philosophies, they will gain a common language and build their own game-changing process.

Accountants and attorneys who service privately-owned companies will find ideas that support and deliver maximum net value.

Investment bankers will see what owners have done to prepare for an exit. Owners will learn how the PABoard process can make their work more productive as they guide owners to the highest exit value.

OWNERS' EXPERIENCES

The last chapter contains the board experiences of owners in their own words. They share how they created and managed their boards and what they learned.

WHAT THE PROFESSIONAL ADVISORY BOARD WANTS TO KNOW

At the end of each chapter is a section entitled "The Advisory Board Wants to Know." These summary sections raise respectful, challenging, and insightful questions. They call for fact-based answers, professional processes and accountability which delivers game-changing results.

APPENDICES

This section contains essential templates, game plans and processes to help you manage your business and your board. Many of these templates are based on the due-diligence process that an investor may use to evaluate your company and its sustainability. The authors have used these tools in many companies to enhance the professionalism and improve the effectiveness of companies.

NEXT STEPS

This PABoard process works. Over the past twenty years, many companies have used it and their valuations have risen substantially. Try the parts that fit you and your company. We hope that the final challenge you have is to choose what you want to do with your valuable company and your freedom.

Acknowledgements

We are grateful for four important sources of learning that have shaped us and this book. The first is the owners of the approximately ninety, privately-held and public companies that we have served as board members. Their energy, determination, resiliency, and hunger for personal growth have been inspirational. We have learned so much from them as they overcame the challenges that they and their companies faced.

We also acknowledge the power of the Vistage International process. For over twenty years, we have had the privilege of interacting with many group chairmen and thousands of members of this executive learning organization. Its powerful process changes lives and enhances owners' effectiveness.

The wisdom of fellow board members has added greatly to our understanding of effective board and management processes. They have also shown us a wide variety of "best practices" for managing companies and how they were applied. Because they have owned or led companies, they know the pressures of being the leader. They bring that real-world knowledge into the boardroom.

Professional service providers such as investment bankers, accountants, lawyers, and wealth advisors continue to be invaluable parts of the learning and support team for the board process. They warn, guide, and protect the owners and their companies. Their knowledge and experience help ensure that the board addresses the right questions and focuses on delivering the highest net value to the owners.

Many people contributed their stories to this book and made it come alive. Thanks to Ted and Teresa Allred, Jerry Bourassa, Larry Braun, Doug Circle, Lori Daniel, Ann Ehringer, Lars Ekstrom, Richard Fontaine, Rick Godber, Dr. Seth Goldberg, Jeff Katke, Allan Keck, Jason Levin, Jeffrey Levine, Anthony Mathews, Phillip Matthews, Stan Megerdichian, Tom Murphy, Don Natenstedt, Thomas Nielsen, Steve Rapattoni, Richard Ross, Jeffrey Sheldon, Neil Sherman, Eric Steinhauer, Eliot Swartz, Keith Swayne, Judy Swayne and Rich White. Thank you for taking the time to write about your experience and share it with those who are interested in building sustainable value.

We want to give special thanks to several colleagues for reading, editing, and commenting on our drafts. They improved the content and effectiveness of the book: Henry DeVries, Richard Fontaine, Ed Freiermuth, Pete Lakey, Jeff Levine, Phillip Matthews, and Don Natenstadt.

There are not enough words to thank Joyce Throgmorton. She suffered through years of writing, rewriting, and editing. Her ability to see the logic or lack of it helped us present ideas in their clearest forms. Her edits have touched every page.

Thanks also to Marc Emmer and Dana Borowka for their advice and insights on the writing and publishing process.

Michael Laney's coaching and encouragement was particularly helpful in shaping the content, focus and style of this book.

Henry DeVries started us on this journey by defining the book's structure, shaping its content, and then guiding us through many of the obstacles to completion. Without his reminder that "perfection is the enemy of excellence," we would still be revising.

Finally, thanks to the CEO members of Vistage 30, chaired by Pete Lakey. They listened patiently to many presentations on this book and gave great advice, encouragement, and caring criticism.

William Hawfield

Co-Founder

The Board Group

John Zaepfel

Co-Founder

The Board Group

Foreword

By Rafael Pastor

At Vistage, we're challenged each and every day to illustrate the power of the CEO peer advisory group experience to someone who has never had the privilege of being part of such a group. Since the benefits are so broad, where does one start?

Let's say you're the chief executive officer of your company. Regardless of how talented or focused your most trusted advisors may be, being the one responsible for making decisions that will affect the entire organization is a completely different challenge. What's more, they understandably bring their own biases and self-interests to the equation. Fellow CEOs who are members of your peer advisory group, on the other hand, aren't looking through the lens of marketing, finance, or HR; they're looking at the whole picture because, like you, it's what they do every day. The empathy that one CEO shares with another is a priceless benefit of the CEO peer advisory experience.

These fellow CEOs tend to ask the hard questions without regard for sacred cows, personal relationships or other organizational/industry blinders. As outsiders, they engage the CEO in the critical exercise of challenging assumptions. It's an eye-opening experience for many CEOs when peers look at a specific challenge through an impartial and fresh lens. And while the CEOs in the group may serve entirely different types of customers in widely varying industries, they share common issues regarding employees, growth, profitability, executive development, technology and uncertainty, just to name a few. The more they exchange ideas and business solutions, the more they realize how much they have in common and how much they can learn from one another.

They talk about their uncertainties and vulnerabilities as well as their aspirations and victories. This display of trust creates an environment where a CEO can be safely open to fierce conversation and bold innovation, when warranted. And while one-to-one executive coaching is a rich complement to the peer advisory experience, there's nothing quite like the power of the group dynamic.

Of course, as CEOs share their challenges and aspirations with their peers, being CEOs as they are, they tend to be serious about holding their peers accountable to make the tough choices and to deliver on their stated courses of action. As I've heard from so many Vistage Chairs and CEO members, this atmosphere of shared accountability may be the most powerful benefit of all.

Most simply put, there is no better way for a CEO to figure out what to do about his/her toughest issues, and then actually do it, than to ask for, listen to, and act upon the experience-based judgment and advice of a group of unbiased and trusted other CEOs. In this community, "been there/done that" can be either comforting or challenging, but it's always valuably useful.

This peer-to-peer experience can also help its participants become highly effective professional board members. From the peer advisory group experience, they have learned:

❖ *Business and personal lessons from the group experience*

❖ *Collaboration and confrontation skills that work with other CEOs*

❖ Insightful questions on business and personal topics

❖ Willingness to bring a broad network of resources to help

❖ Skills and ideas gathered from speakers and workshops

❖ Understanding and appreciation of a variety of industry and business models

❖ The deep understanding of what ownership and the "corner office" means

Vistage members are well practiced at participating in a group process that often challenges their assumptions and ideas. They appreciate honest, direct appraisals and caring confrontation. Because they can bring that mindset and style to corporate board meetings, they can generate a board dynamic that's lively, collegial and highly productive.

For a deep dive into the complimentary process of the professional advisory board, I invite you to explore the pages of Bill and John's book. They cover just about anything you need to know about whether joining or creating a professional advisory board is right for you and how to maximize the experience once you do.

Bill and John are participants, leaders, and speakers with Vistage and other peer advisory groups across the country. They lead many professional advisory and fiduciary boards. They know what they're talking about, as they share their years of experience in this book with the same generosity they bring to their board work. It's the next best thing to experiencing a board yourself.

Rafael Pastor

Chief Executive Officer

Vistage International

The Authors

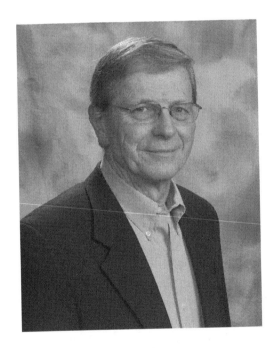

WILLIAM HAWFIELD

Bill Hawfield is a professional manager, international speaker, business owner and a recognized, board process authority. After thirteen years at General Mills, where he was a division president, he left and started the Penguin's Frozen Yogurt franchise company. The retail chain grew rapidly to 130 stores before it was sold to a French company.

Hawfield has served on more than thirty five boards, both fiduciary and advisory in a wide variety of industries, including distribution, construction, manufacturing, aerospace, financial services, consulting, insurance, and food service. He has served as non-executive chairman, lead director, and a member of audit and compensation committees.

He is a member of the National Association of Corporate Directors and has completed the NACD director certification program. He has presented to the Family Business Boards workshops for the NACD and is a faculty member in their Family Business Leadership forum in Los Angeles.

He is an international speaker for Vistage, an organization comprising 15,000 CEOs worldwide. His topics are "Personal and Business Success" and "Getting to Your End Game." He is the co-founder of The Board Group, which creates and manages advisory boards for privately-owned companies. He is also CEO of Hillcrest Associates.

His education includes a degree in Physics from Virginia Military Institute, an MBA in management from the University of Virginia, and twenty-five years of Vistage International membership.

JOHN ZAEPFEL

John Zaepfel has had a varied and successful business career as a CEO, board chairman, and CEO coach. During the fifteen years he spent as a President/CEO, he founded CPG International as part of an LBO in the fine art, graphic art, engineering, drafting, and media supplies field with thirteen domestic and international facilities. CPG was sold to financial buyers.

He has served on fifty-two public and private company boards and currently serves on numerous public, private statutory and advisory boards, chairing several as a non-executive chairman.

He has served as a public company director for Ideal School Supply, Varitronics, The Troy Group, Hi-Shear Technology, and RemedyTemp, Inc. He served as chairman of the board of Accordia of Southern California. He has assisted as a board member in four public offerings, several change-of-control transactions, and has chaired two public audit committees that installed Sarbanes-Oxley requirements.

John is a past member of the Young Presidents Organization and is currently a member of the Chief Executives Organization.

He has worked with the members of Vistage International for over twenty years as a group chairman and as a speaker.

He is the co-founder of The Board Group, which creates boards and manages advisory boards for privately-owned companies. He is also CEO of The Zaepfel Group.

Zaepfel is a graduate of the University of Washington and holds an MBA from the Marshall School of Business at the University of Southern California.

Part I:

The Middle-Market Company Valuation Challenge

Chapter 1

The Five Challenges to Building Sustainable Value

*"A trap is only a trap if you don't know about it.
If you know about it, it's a challenge."*

China Miéville, King Rat

This is an actual situation of middle-market valuation challenges. The names and industry have been changed to protect the wealthy.

The CEO and co-owners of an appliance manufacturing business, AppCo, were highly frustrated. Sales had been declining, and because earnings were low, there was no value in the business.

The partners were well matched in good times. One was "Mister Inside" and in charge of operations and finances. The other partner was "Mister Outside." He provided high energy to the sales and customer acquisition effort. In tough times, like today, they could not agree on anything. Decision making was slow and inconsistent. Anger showed in staff meetings.

Both owners wanted to sell the business, but neither saw a way to change what they had or how to get beyond the day-to-day bickering and poor results. They were trapped.

They decided to bring in outside input and guidance. They formed an advisory board and began periodic meetings. They selected one of the board members to be the non-executive chair to run the meetings to ensure that they followed board process, best practices.

The first board meetings focused on "Where are you today?" and "Where do you want to go?" The advisory board chairman required the owners to discuss their differences in front of the other board members. The owners realized that they wanted roughly the same outcome: sell the business for $75 million in three to five years. They agreed that they were a long way from that valuation today. Now they had to agree on how to get to the future that they agreed on.

The board guided them to changing the business game they were playing. They had to increase revenues and create long-term sustainability. The board pushed them to understand profitability by product segment, enter new markets, and focus on a new technology. Board meetings required fact-based decisions, professional measurements, and accountability for actions agreed to. Earnings began to improve.

The board convinced the owners to hire an experienced CEO. Together, the owners and the new CEO developed a credible strategic plan. The board approved the plan. The plan and the results began to attract potential investors.

One of the board members introduced an investment banker who specialized in companies of their size and who fit the personality of the owners. The investment banker and the CEO crafted an exit plan that the board approved. Two years later, the company sold for ten times earnings which was 30 percent above their goal. The owners had overcome the five challenges of a middle-market company. They were happy. They had achieved their exit plan.

LEARNINGS FROM THE APPCO STORY

❖ *Partners will take action to deal with the conflict after some pain.*

❖ *The owners defined the outcome they wanted: to sell their company at their price and on their terms.*

❖ *They brought in outsider board members to help implement the process.*

❖ *The big step was hiring the right CEO to run the business.*

❖ *They agreed on a strategic plan and exit plan.*

❖ *An investment banker informed the owners about what a buyer would value, how to prepare for sale, and how to go to market.*

❖ *The owners created much more cash value than they expected.*

Five Challenges to Creating **Peak Sustainable Value**

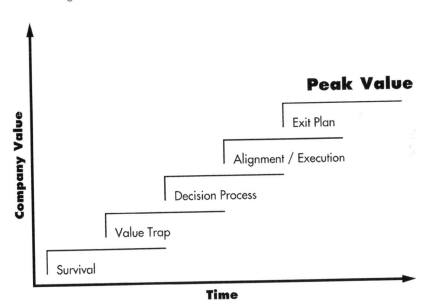

THE FIVE CHALLENGES

The authors have seen CEOs and owners struggle to meet the challenges to building sustainable value in their companies. These challenges are shown as a progression from low value at the survival stage to a high value exit plan at the top of the stairs.

CHALLENGE NUMBER ONE—FIGHTING FOR SURVIVAL

Between 2008 and 2011, 11,740 significant middle-market companies filed for Chapter 11 bankruptcy. Whole industries related to residential and commercial construction were decimated. Businesses that depended heavily on state or federal discretionary spending saw revenue streams disappear. Retail book chains closed from loss of sales to Internet retailers like Amazon. Empty buildings were everywhere.

Many of the companies that comprise these statistics did not see what was coming. Then, and now, middle-market company leadership and management often fall into a trap of working *in* the business but not *on* the business. They continually fail to ask the question "what if?" and do not properly plan for the contingencies they might face.

Survival challenges are both external and internal. External challenges come from economic changes, marketplace dynamics, competitors' actions, government policies, customer departures, or pricing challenges. Internal challenges usually involve poor strategic direction, weak teams, high employee turnover, inadequate systems, poor decisions and lack of financial resources.

People challenges involve hiring, firing, retaining the management team, and improving workforce efficiency.

Systems challenges come from the cost of keeping up with technology changes and designing a knowledge-based infrastructure that can give management actionable information.

Internal decision-making processes are often weak. The complexity of the business environment has outpaced the owner's ability and his company's processes to manage effectively and efficiently.

Financial challenges may be shrinking margins, deteriorating balance sheets, or inability to generate working capital. The evaporation of working capital will sound the death knell of a business. Running out of cash means you are "out of options."

Any of these challenges, when coupled with a weak economy and aggressive competitors, can kill a company.

Challenge Number Two—Escaping the Value Creation Trap

According to *The Wall Street Journal*, the companies in the S&P 500 lost over $7 trillion dollars in value from the end of 2007 to 2010. Middle-market companies were hit just as hard. An owner may now find himself or herself trapped in the company. Often the owner cannot see how the company's value can be increased doing business in the same outmoded model. The company does not have enough value for the owner to sell and retire.

How can the owner devise a new strategy that will build enough value over the next three to five years? What new internal processes and disciplines must be added? What team can make this happen? How can the owner get out of this trap and gain his or her freedom?

Owners and management often fail to design strategies that will create value that is attractive to lenders, investors, or buyers. In other words, they "fail to plan" to create sustainable value.

CHALLENGE NUMBER THREE—MAKING CONSISTENTLY GOOD DECISIONS

All companies' structures and performances are the result of past management decisions. To paraphrase Peter Drucker, when he started his work, he thought that management was responsible for 85 percent of the problems in companies. After years of research, he found that the number is approximately 95 percent.

The typical middle-market business owner is alone. No one in his organization is a true peer. He cannot tell others of his real fears. There is no forum to truly vet his thinking. Without challenge or input, his decisions are often not optimal.

As private companies grow, many owners tend to shy away from seeking external counsel. They believe they have the answers. Owners make decisions and design strategies in a vacuum, fearful of revealing the supposed secrets of their business. They fight for short-term survival instead of long-term success. Decisions are embedded in the corner office and not vetted internally or externally. Owners make decisions either too quickly or too slowly. Often, there is no active strategic plan or planning process. If this plan is absent, then decisions are made without a clear view of their impact on future value.

Challenge Number Four—Improving Alignment and Execution

A fourth challenge is company alignment, both internally and externally. Many owners are not aligned on strategy, investment options, compensation, and other critical areas. Family-owned businesses may not have "one voice" from the owners to management. The result is a management team that is out of sync on company goals, purpose, business philosophy, and even ethics. This misalignment leads to inefficiency, false starts, misspent capital, products that add little value, and management turnover. The outcome is weaker financial performance and lower value.

Challenge Number Five—Developing a Viable Exit Strategy

An old adage says, "It is easier to get into business than it is to get out of business." Middle-market companies usually fail to focus on how to create sustainable value. They do not know how to align the company's capabilities and position it to appeal to targeted investors and acquirers. Planning a viable exit strategy forces companies to ask, "What is attractive about the business, who would be attracted to it, and what needs to change so that it is more valuable?"

These companies often disregard the notion of scalability, brand equity, bankable management teams, and recurring revenues. These are just a few of the important factors in designing an attractive exit strategy. Owners might not choose to exit a business, but they should know the factors that build sustainable value. The challenge is to have a plan for building sustainable value that can be measured, managed, and executed.

If the exit strategy leads to the sale of the business, owners must decide the acceptable price and terms. They must be prepared emotionally to sell if their terms are met.

TRAPPED

The unwillingness or inability of company owners to deal with the five challenges results in "the trap."

It is not unusual for CEOs and owners who feel trapped to say they were too busy running a business to think about leaving it. The irony is that for the vast majority of companies, considerable planning goes into creating a business launch; however, scant attention is paid to building sustainable value or designing an attractive exit plan.

Here are some characteristics of middle-market companies whose owners are "trapped":

* Unpredictable earnings
* Unreliable revenue forecasts
* Sales concentration in a few customers or products
* Deteriorating gross and net margins
* Knowledge retained solely in the corner office
* Weak management teams
* Systems and processes lagging behind competition
* Commodity market positioning with little differentiation

Many owners have recognized these traps and have turned to outside advice from others who have managed through them.

As mentioned in the quotation at the beginning of the chapter, if you can recognize a trap, it is no longer a trap. It becomes a challenge. The five challenges were:

1. *Fighting for Survival*
2. *Escaping the Value Creation Trap*
3. *Making Consistently Good Decisions*
4. *Improving Alignment and Execution*
5. *Developing a Viable Exit Strategy*

How to Meet the Challenges

Overcome the challenges with a strong internal team supported by an advisory board and the governance process it brings to the company. The authors have created an effective advisory board process called the professional advisory board process or PABoard process.

The PABoard Process Defined

As the French philosopher Voltaire said, "If you want to have a conversation with me, first define your terms." Several terms require definition because they are central to this book and our discussion:

- ❖ *Sustainable value*
- ❖ *Middle Market*
- ❖ *Owners*
- ❖ *Professional Advisory Board (PABoard)*

SUSTAINABLE VALUE

Sustainable value is more than a multiple of earnings. It is more than just the equity or book value. It is not the liquidation value. It is the value that an investor or buyer would place on the company without the founder on the team.

> ### SUSTAINABLE VALUE
> THE QUANTIFIABLE TRUST THAT INVESTORS HAVE
> IN A COMPANY'S LONG-TERM PROFITABILITY,
> VALUE AND SUCCESS.

When a buyer or investor evaluates your company, he looks at five primary components of the business model:

1. EBITDA (Earnings Before Interest, Taxes, Depreciation and Amortization) performance and gross margin strength

2. Effective business disciplines

3. Long-term attractiveness of the markets served

4. Excellent CEO and team who create a strong culture

5. Predictable revenues from products and customer relationships

Sustainable Value Model Overview

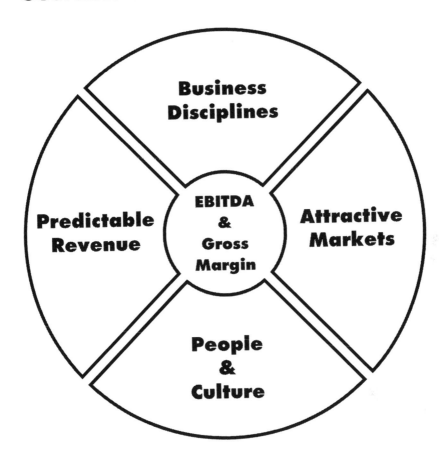

The buyer purchases all of these components when he buys a company. Together they can add up to trust in the future of the business. If the buyer's trust is high in each of these sectors, he will assign a high value to your company and pay a strong price. Congratulations—you have created real sustainable value. This model will be explored and its components revealed as you move through this book.

> **EXCEPTIONAL SUSTAINABLE VALUE**
> SUSTAINABLE VALUE THAT IS MUCH HIGHER THAN THE
> AVERAGE VALUE OF A COMPARABLE COMPANY IN YOUR
> MARKET AS MEASURED BY HIGH MULTIPLES OF **EBITDA.**

EXCEPTIONAL SUSTAINABLE VALUE

If the norm for valuation of companies in your industry is four times earnings, then "exceptional sustainable value" could be five or six times earnings. The goal of this book is to create the highest sustainable value possible in privately-owned, middle-market companies.

MIDDLE MARKET

The definition of middle market is elastic. The National Centre for the Middle Market at Ohio State University says, "America has around 197,000 medium-sized firms defined as those with annual revenues between $10M and $1B. They employ over 40M people and produce about one-third of private-sector GDP. Some 82% survived the dark years of 2007-2010 and added 2.2M jobs. They tend to be privately owned: 31% by a family, and a further 40% by some combination of private equity and family.

OWNERS

The authors have chosen to use the term *owners* to denote those that own the shares of a company. The term encompasses shareholders of all classes and types, voting and non-voting. These owners could be the CEO, family members, trusts, private investors, management, or other shareholders.

PROFESSIONAL ADVISORY BOARD (PABOARD) PROCESS

This process is led by an advisory board that serves at the plea-sure of the owner. Outside members who are former CEOs and key executives bring learning, contacts, and constructive criticism to the owner and his or her teams.

The PABoard process is a governance process created by the authors to build sustainable value. The key elements are attracting board members with the right set of skills and experience, manag-ing the expectation and accountability process, and setting the right structure for growth and sustainability.

If the owners of these middle-market companies execute the pro-cess, they will define the outcomes they want, make excellent deci-sions, increase their opportunities to build strong companies, and get the outcomes, end games, that they want.

The Advisory Board Wants to Know:

1. How do you measure the value of your business today? What is that value? Is it enough?

2. Looking at the five challenges to building sustainable value, which ones are most difficult for you and your team today? How can you meet these challenges?

3. If your company were being run by an outside, professional manager, what three changes would he make to build value?

4. What is the one decision you must make that will have the biggest impact on the future value of your company?

5. What is your exit strategy? At the current profit rate of your company, when would you have the freedom to exit or move out of your operating role?

6. Who would want to buy or invest in your company? What would they value most?

CHAPTER 2

Overcoming the Middle-Market Challenges

*"The things that got you to where you are today
are not the things that will get you to the future."*
Peter Drucker

This is a story of game over!

ABC Corporation, a major distributor for high-end, plumbing hardware manufacturers, was twenty-five years old with $75 Million in gross revenues. It was reasonably profitable compared to its competitors and had a unique competitive position in its local market.

The founder decided to step away from day-to-day operations. The second generation moved up to take a more active role in management.

To ensure that the transition to the next generation went smoothly, the company's CPA and corporate attorney suggested an advisory board to help professionalize the company and prepare for an eventual exit.

The owners and management decided not to assemble an advisory board. They decided to tackle the transition and strategic issues alone. Competitive price pressure increased from the big boxes, and regional competitors compressed their margins. Owners and management could not agree on the strategies to meet these challenges. Alignment between owners and management began to evaporate. Decision making was stymied. Actions were reactive and slow. Survival was now in question.

The owners were trapped. Value was deteriorating rapidly. Equity investors and strategic buyers who had expressed interested before, now began to disappear.

In a desperate move, management decided to expand regionally to grow revenues, thinking this was a key factor to increase company value. They added warehouse capacity and increased inventory. Sales in the new geographic areas grew slowly. Inventory accumulated. Operating expenses ballooned, and working capital declined. Debt compared to equity increased to 4.75 to 1. Auditors raised questions and expressed concern. The bank called the loan.

The company was eventually liquidated. The shareholders lost all their equity.

LESSONS LEARNED

What can we learn from this real life, undesirable outcome? The major initiatives that a PABoard would have started for ABC, Inc., are:

- ❖ A smooth transition from founder to new leaders. There would have been coaching for the next generation for several years before the founder stepped back.

- ❖ Alignment and professional decision making on the critical challenges between the owners.

- ❖ An exit plan to assure consistent, focused execution.

❖ Accountability assigned and key actions tracked.

❖ Bank negotiations. An advisory board member with financial experience would have assisted the CFO. Bank covenant violations would have been addressed and actions taken to ease the bank's concerns.

❖ Tight cash and cost controls. Processes and board oversight would have ensured cash was managed well.

Why Advisory Boards Are Formed

If you asked owners who have advisory boards why they formed them, they would give you many reasons, such as:

"I want to make consistently good decisions, but I have no peers to talk to or to tell me if I am headed in the wrong direction."

"The world is getting more and more complex. I cannot see all the problems or opportunities. I need experienced, talented people to guide me."

"We needed to change the way we did business. If we had not, we would have failed. We needed outside ideas and strong coaches to push us to change."

"As partners, we were in total disagreement. We needed referees we respected."

"We wanted to sell the business at the best terms possible. It took three years, but the board got us there by pushing us to design an exit plan and make the tough decisions."

In the end, the short answer to "why a board?" is, these owners formed a board because they wanted to create sustainable value in their business. They might not have articulated that answer themselves, but they knew they wanted a strong company, with great earnings, a solid balance sheet, excellent people, controls, accountability that worked, and predictable results.

They wanted to sleep well at night knowing that their future was secure. They wanted to feel good about the company they owned and have the freedom to play the role they wanted to play in their business.

WHAT BUSINESS OUTCOMES DO ADVISORY BOARDS DELIVER?

Most owners of middle-market companies are hands-on, action-oriented people. They want tangible business results from a board process. Here are several outcomes they want from their advisory board:

- ❖ **Survive.** Get the professional guidance and resources needed from outside that will lead to making the right changes, quickly.

- ❖ **Grow sales and profitability.** Generate innovative ideas for sales and instill financial discipline to build sustainable value.

- ❖ **Prepare their company for sale.** Identify potential buyers and ensure the company is positioned to be an attractive acquisition target.

- ❖ **Provide wise counsel to the CEO.** Help him or her confront difficult ethical, personnel, or customer issues.

- ❖ **Strengthen the organizational structure.** Assist the CEO in selecting game breakers for key positions and designing a meaningful succession plan.

- ❖ **Raise equity capital.** Work with management to prepare the plans, design the measurement processes and deliver the performance that will attract outside investors. Make introductions to the right investment partners.

❖ **Support the CEO.** *Mentor the CEO by helping him focus on what is important, coach him on his decision-making process, and enhance his leadership skills. Hold him accountable for doing what he says he will do.*

❖ **Mitigate shareholder issues.** *Provide unbiased counsel and coaching to the owners, family members, and the CEO.*

❖ **Define a sustainable growth strategy.** *Identify alliances and acquisitions that will augment the growth targets.*

❖ **Bring in breakthrough strategic thinking.** *Devise an innovation strategy to grow the business.*

❖ **Build a strong culture.** *Move from a lifestyle to a professionally managed environment.*

❖ **Increase accountability.** *Provide a reporting atmosphere for management to improve tactical and strategic execution.*

❖ **Results.** *Show positive, reproducible and predictable outcomes.*

If the advisory board delivers these outcomes, it will have enabled the company and its owners to overcome the challenges defined in Chapter One.

What Is a Professional Advisory Board?

A professional advisory board is "professional" because of the qualifications of the people on the board and the process they follow.

The members are from inside and outside the company. The insiders are the CEO and the owner if they are not the same person. They represent the wishes and values of the owners, the knowledge of the industry, the operations of the business and the people in their company. It is their vision of the future that defines the outcomes of the board's work.

The outsiders are experienced and talented business leaders whose skills, experiences, and connections fit the long-term needs of the company. They are independent. They are current or former CEOs and senior executives who bring a set of values, experience, and professional structure to a private company. Many have served on public boards and bring that discipline to the process. Their style is to question and give their advice with full respect for the owners' values and desired future.

The PABoard process that the authors have created is an effective and disciplined process. It ensures that there is a professional meeting process, preparation, and follow through. Here is a representation of the functions of a PABoard arranged in order of importance.

The Importance of Board Functions

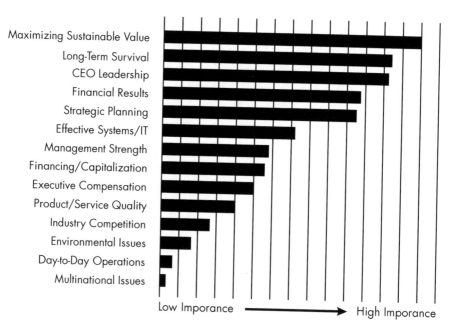

Maximizing Sustainable Value
Long-Term Survival
CEO Leadership
Financial Results
Strategic Planning
Effective Systems/IT
Management Strength
Financing/Capitalization
Executive Compensation
Product/Service Quality
Industry Competition
Environmental Issues
Day-to-Day Operations
Multinational Issues

Low Imporance   ⟶   High Imporance

By giving proper weight to these functions in their agendas and their thinking, the owners and the board are working *on* the future value of the business and not just *in* the operations of the business. The board asks management to define the issues well, gather the relevant information, collaborate with a team to develop alternatives, present and defend their conclusions to the board, and then execute efficiently and effectively.

The process is guided by the outside board members who add outside wisdom, creativity, contacts, and a healthy dose of constructive criticism. The board coaches the team to establish measurements and then monitors the results associated with the decisions, actions, and outcomes.

This is the essence of how boards help their owners, CEOs, and senior management overcome the Five Challenges and build sustainable value.

WHAT A PROFESSIONAL ADVISORY BOARD IS NOT

To understand what a PABoard is, requires an understanding of what it is not.

It is not:

- ❖ A gathering of country-club cronies of the owners
- ❖ A group of "insiders" such as the family accountant, lawyer, or family members
- ❖ A statutory board with fiduciary responsibilities, liabilities or authority
- ❖ A binding legal obligation for the owners

All private corporations are required by state laws to have a fiduciary board. Most middle-market companies have a passive fiduciary board that meets infrequently to approve resolutions or sign documents such as board resolutions and minutes.

The responsibility of a fiduciary board of directors, whether it is active or passive, is to oversee the management of a corporation as it undertakes business. It determines the general policies that govern the business' operations. The board is legally bound to represent the long-term financial interests of the shareholders, private or public, by providing governance, guidance, strategic oversight, care, and loyalty.

Comparison of a Fiduciary and an Advisory Board

Governance Factor	Fiduciary Board	Advisory Board
Legal Authority	Fiduciary with full legal authority and responsibility	Advisory with no legal authority or liability
CEO Management	CEO reports to the board and it has the power to fire him or her	CEO/owner is advised by the board
Personal Legal Exposure	High, defined by fiduciary law	Low, because of no legal authority
Ability to Create Change	High, using statutory authority	High, using influence and persuasion

The legal requirements of a PABoard are much less stringent than a fiduciary board, although the processes are similar. Most of the differences between a fiduciary board and an advisory board can be grouped in six factors:

❖ **Control.** Unlike a fiduciary board, an advisory board does not have a legal authority or fiduciary responsibility for the organization. An advisory board will review and provide suggestions about policies, compensation and financial matters, but cannot pass a board resolution to enforce action. They create change through influence and persuasion.

❖ **Responsibility.** Many of the responsibilities of a fiduciary board and an advisory board are the same; however, the main difference is that a fiduciary board is legally bound to manage the CEO and the organization while an advisory board is in place to advise and coach. The advisory board, however, should pay attention to the safeguarding of company assets, ensuring reliability and integrity of information; compliance with laws, regulations, and policies; and the cost effectiveness of resources.

❖ **Risk.** Because a fiduciary is someone controlling assets for another party, with legal authority and duty to make responsible decisions regarding the other party, the law holds them to a higher standard of accountability than an advisory board member.

❖ **Process.** Fiduciary boards follow a formal process designed to safeguard the interests of shareholders. A PABoard follows a very similar process, but the focus is on mentoring the CEO and management and driving excellent decision making. This process helps the team prepare for a possible transition to a fiduciary board model.

❖ **Rewards.** The maxim "the greater the risk, the greater the rewards" holds true with boards. An advisory board costs less to operate than a fiduciary board because there is very little legal exposure for the members. As with fiduciary boards, a shareholder/owner may offer members some participation in the value that is created in the PABoard process so that the board is highly focused on building company value.

❖ **Legal structure.** *Advisory boards, unlike fiduciary boards, can be terminated easily. Their legal standing in the company is similar to that of a consultant; however, the company usually has an indemnification and non-disclosure agreement with the members.*

WHERE ARE WE HEADED?

An owner's future does not need to be limited by the Five Challenges. The PABoard is a game-changing process that leads to consistently making good decisions, taking effective actions and building sustainable value. This book will help business owners work in their businesses in the ways they choose and get the outcomes, end games, that they want.

REAL GAME, REAL BOARD

"AN ADVISORY BOARD IS ESSENTIAL TO GROWING A LONG-TERM, SUSTAINABLE BUSINESS. WE HAVE HAD A BOARD FOR OVER THIRTY YEARS. I CAN'T THINK OF NOT HAVING ONE. ALL BUSINESS PROCESSES ARE IMPROVED FROM PLANNING ALL THE WAY TO CLIENT SATISFACTION AND RETENTION. FROM AN IDEA TO AN EXIT PLAN, THE PROCESSES ARE IMPROVED TO A MUCH HIGHER LEVEL WITH A HIGHLY FUNCTIONAL ADVISORY BOARD. EVRYONE GROWS. EVERYONE BENEFITS.

GARY BRINDERSON, CHAIRMAN, BRINDERSON HOLDINGS

The Advisory Board Wants to Know:

Consider for a few moments how a professional advisory board could assist your business in overcoming challenges and creating sustainable value. Here are several questions.

1. What are the three to five most important issues or opportunities that your company is facing today?

2. What are the consequences of not making great decisions on these issues?

3. What are the skills or experience that your company needs to resolve these issues or gain greatly from the opportunities? Do you have these skills and experience in your company or are there gaps?

4. When you review the list of outcomes that advisory boards deliver on page 18, which three would be most valuable to you?

Part II:

The Professional Advisory Board Solution

CHAPTER 3

Building a Winning Board

"If everyone is thinking alike, then someone is not thinking."
General George Patton

HOW TO FIND, ATTRACT, AND DEVELOP A WINNING TEAM

A Japanese proverb says, "None of us is as smart as all of us." Operating a business is difficult and increasingly complex. No one person has all the answers for managing that complexity so that it creates greater value. It takes a diverse, smart, and dedicated organization, as well as a carefully selected group of professional board members to build sustainable value. This team is focused on delivering the "win" that the owners and shareholders have defined.

As part of the "winning team," a winning board must have members who have the right skills, experience, and style to fit the owners, the company's situation, and the game plan for winning. When these board members have been found, attracted, and become committed to the company, they can be organized into an effective and highly functioning professional team.

PROFESSIONAL ADVISORY BOARDS ARE ATTRACTIVE

If an experienced businessperson wants to join a board today, he or she might consider joining the board of a publicly-traded company. Unfortunately, directors of public boards, large and small, are being sued personally for failing in their fiduciary responsibility. Many qualified board members are concerned about taking on the legal responsibility and exposure of governing a public company. Because of the increasing risk, public company board members have told the authors that they are spending more of their board time on covering their legal risks and those of the company and less on issues that could increase the company's value.

The structure and process of the PABoard has a special attraction for seasoned business leaders compared to serving on fiduciary boards. The legal structure offers less risk for a PABoard member because of the word "advisory." The advisory board gives advice. It does not have statuary authority or responsibility. The owner or the CEO can take the advice or, like a consultant's advice, they can ignore it. The fiduciary responsibility lies with the owners and officers of the company. This advisory structure opens the agenda to spending less time on oversight and security and more on issues and opportunities.

This advisory board structure enables an owner of a middle-market company to attract highly credentialed business leaders who may have considerable net worth, great networks and larger company experience. Because their personal liability is very low, they spend the majority of their board time dealing with real business issues. They are in a collaborative, "non-legalized" environment. The board can still help the owners create real change in their companies and their lives through their influence and advice. And, they can be well compensated financially and emotionally for their time.

REASONS FOR SERVING

The recruitment of PABoard members should be pursued in a systematic manner, just as you would pursue hiring any top executive for the firm. Here are several non-financial reasons why highly respected, successful people join a PABoard:

- ❖ **Respect.** Potential board members will join a board because they like and respect the CEO. The board member and the CEO need to have mutual respect. Mutual respect goes a long way toward fostering a healthy relationship between board members and the CEO. It is necessary to facilitate efficient and effective execution.

- ❖ **Honor.** They are honored to be on the CEO's board. Being a board member is recognition of their experience and capabilities.

- ❖ **Coach.** They want to coach and help the CEO and members of the management team. Mentoring someone and watching them grow can be tremendously satisfying. For some, it is a form of payback in honor of those people who mentored them along in their career. If a board member helps the CEO succeed, that helps all the employees and the owners live better lives.

- ❖ **Meaning.** Board work adds meaning and enjoyment to their lives. Your company's mission statement or vision may resonate with prospective board members. They want to serve a cause they believe in.

- ❖ **Achievement.** They want to help the CEO define and attain his or her goals for the company. These goals are then the measures of achievement for the CEO and the company. Board members are business people who are passionate about defining, playing, and winning the game of business.

If the candidates are there for the right reasons, then they need to bring the right stuff to the meetings in a way that will be accepted by the CEO and the owners.

THE RIGHT STUFF

The "right stuff" is defined in the context of what outcomes the owners want and what the company needs to deliver those outcomes. If these two areas are defined, then the owners can move to selecting board members who will add the right value. Consider three sets of criteria when recruiting for your board members:

- ❖ **Experience.** With a clear vision and understanding of the success drivers that will deliver that vision, the owners can evaluate the additional experience the management team and owners need to achieve success. The owners can then attract executives who have "been there" and can use that experience to guide the team in its decision making. Examples of valuable experience are: deep industry experience, history of successfully managing larger companies, experience working for a major competitor, or knowledge of a market segment that your company wants to enter.

- ❖ **Skills.** The advisory board also should bring functional skills and knowledge that support the company's needs. Middle-market companies often do not have the level of skills that can manage a larger, more complex company. For instance, specific financial skills may be needed to help the company strengthen its financial structure, confidently project earnings and cash flow, and deal with banks and outside investors. A board member, who was once the CFO of a larger company, would be a powerful coach for the CFO and the CEO.

- ❖ **Fit.** A professional advisory board needs to be a collection of like-minded individuals who are committed to working together in harmony with the owners, the CEO, and their fellow board members. They should have different styles and personalities, but the mix needs to be a winning team that works well together.

BOARD CRITERIA SCORECARD

In the sourcing and selection process, the shareholders and CEO should prepare a list of criteria for the board positions. This listing and rating of these criteria help everyone agree on what skills, experience, and fit are important in these outsiders. It is also a scorecard that each member of the selection team can use so that he or she can effectively compare and discuss the candidates. An example of a criteria scorecard is shown below:

Candidate Criteria	Importance (1-10)	Score (A-F)
Experience		
1. Our industry		
2. Larger companies		
3. CEO and leadership positions		
4. Prior boards		
Skills		
1. Understands financial statements		
2. Leadership		
3. Strategic and long-term thinker		
4. Technology		
Fit or Character		
1. Fits our culture		
2. Respectful		
3. Time available		
4. Good reputation and high integrity		
Comments and Notes		

When the evaluations of each candidate by each interviewer are completed, create a comparison table. Place the criteria on the vertical axis and the candidates' names across the top horizontal axis. Then add the ratings given for each candidate for each criterion by each interviewer. Look for at least one candidate who has scored well in each of the criteria to ensure that you have covered all the attributes for a complete board.

Jerry Bourassa, Chairman of the Board and partner at McGladrey LLP, a certified public accounting firm, advises his clients that having the right board is one of the basic building blocks for an organization. "A strategic advisory board helps a company get focused on doing the right things to drive business growth and organizational effectiveness," says Bourassa. "It serves as a sounding board for owners and management. It increases their comfort level for making tough decisions. A strong board also gives outsiders, such as banks or private equity groups, confidence that the company has a strong governance process. This can make the organization more attractive when it is positioning itself for a sale or seeking capital to grow the business."

SETTING UP THE BOARD FOR SUCCESS—SKILL SETS

"Creating an advisory board is a terrific way to strengthen and grow your business," says Jill Kaufman, program manager of the Advisory Board Council, an economic development program with funding from Orange County, Florida.

Kaufman continues, "Behind every great board success is a well-defined board process. But you need the right individual skill sets on the board to make the process highly effective. The following are some attributes of what the board members should possess to effectively assist a middle-market private company grow and succeed.

Strategic Planning. They should be well versed in setting strategic direction and have experience in growing a company to a monetary transaction.

Goal Setting. Board members need to be well versed in establishing goals and assisting the CEO in clarifying outcomes while developing specific action measurements for the management team.

Prioritization. They must be able to assimilate alternatives and help management establish focus and clarity of action.

Coaching. They need to be able to pass their knowledge along through proper coaching and mentoring. They inspire CEOs to greater leadership heights through their own positive examples. They help CEOs get through the tough times and act as cheerleaders when appropriate.

Assessing the Team. Board members who have a knack for assessing management team members and new-hire prospects are invaluable. By exposing the board to the management team, the CEO will get invaluable and objective feedback on direct reports. Advisory boards also have the responsibility to give guidance in the delicate matter of CEO succession. "A board has the willingness to bring the subject up, in a supportive and patient way," says John L. Ward, a professor at Northwestern University's Kellogg School of Management and author of *Creating Effective Boards for Private Enterprises*. "Then once it's on the table, it creates a forum of safety for the conversation."

Confrontation. Board members have to be willing to challenge CEOs and management on the key decision areas in the business.

Financial Acumen. Board members should have a strong understanding of the financial reporting and controls in a well-managed company. It is always helpful to have at least one board member who has functional expertise and experience in the financial area.

Industry Knowledge. At least one board member should have deep knowledge of the company's industry. Every industry is changing rapidly, which makes it even more essential to have a longer-term review of possible trends and changes.

Functional Expertise. Each board member should have meaningful experience in a functional area in order to round out a team approach. "Most boards really need someone who is skilled at marketing," says Bob Shepard, director of Score, at the Disney Entrepreneur Center in Orlando, who has served as a member of advisory boards. "The problem with many, many companies is not understanding what true marketing needs are versus sales."

Transactions. It is very important to have advisory board members who have been through transactions—selling to a strategic buyer, negotiating equity capital, or preparing and executing a public offering."

WHERE TO FIND THEM

Where do you find great board members?

First, look for seasoned CEOs and "C" level executives and persons who are already board members. Use your knowledge and contacts.

Second, the CEO or other owners may know qualified professionals who want to help the company succeed and who may meet some of the criteria mentioned earlier. Often owners will trust someone they know. This may lead to a good candidate, but it may also lead to bringing in associates who will not challenge the owner's thinking. Evaluate everyone on his or her merits, not on familiarity.

Third, dream a little. Think of business leaders in your industry or in a company that you respect. Make a list of these people, and network with others to find a way to reach them. Retired executives from public or private companies who have had success in the company's vertical market make good candidates. He or she could be a former customer, competitor, or vendor.

Fourth, consider connecting with an excellent CEO development group. Two well-respected organizations are Vistage International and Young Presidents' Organization (YPO). Both organizations are international leaders in management development and group processes that develop CEOs and organizations. Another group to consider is The Entrepreneurs Organization (EO), which includes younger CEOs. Here is a synopsis of each organization.

VISTAGE INTERNATIONAL

With more than 15,000 members, Vistage International (previously known as TEC in the United States) describes itself as the world's foremost chief executive leadership peer organization. Vistage's Executive Leadership Program provides monthly peer workshops, one-on-one business coaching, speaker presentations from hundreds of top industry experts, social networking, and an extensive online content library of articles, best practices, podcasts, and webinars.

Today, Vistage International and its global affiliates operate in sixteen countries. Vistage members meet in small groups every month under the same guiding principles: to help one another make better decisions, achieve better results, and enhance their lives. In these groups, they learn to challenge their fellow CEOs with respect and caring. They see a wide array of companies, leaders, and issues. The Vistage process is a CEO peer advisory group process and that experience translates to good professional advisory board dynamics.

TEC Canada and TEC Wisconsin are affiliates of Vistage Internaional. Their missions, processes, structure and meeting formats are very similar. All are CEO peer advisory groups lead by trained facilitators and coaches called Chairman.

YOUNG PRESIDENTS' ORGANIZATION

Young Presidents' Organization (YPO), founded in 1950 in New York, is a powerful international network of young global leaders. It connects more than 18,000 members in local chapters in one hundred nations. The members learn and exchange ideas that address the challenges young leaders face today.

All members are age fifty or younger. YPO's purpose is to help build "Better Leaders, Through Education and Idea Exchange" among its peer members and their families.

Members of World Presidents' Organization (WPO) and Chief Executives Organization (CEO), both graduate organizations of YPO, combine corporate responsibility and personal public service to create contributions in the communities where they live and work. As lifetime leaders, WPO and CEO members contribute in the fields of corporate governance, public service, and educational advancement.

OTHER CEO ORGANIZATIONS

The Entrepreneurs' Organization—for entrepreneurs only—is a network of more than 7,300 business owners in forty-two countries. This organization enables entrepreneurs to learn from each other in order to support business success and a better personal life. The average member is forty years old with annual company revenues of $17.3 million (US).

BENEFITS OF CEO ORGANIZATION MEMBERS

Why do the authors recommend business leaders from these "members only" groups of CEOs for advisory board work?

- They have given and taken advice from other CEOs for years. They have the ability to work with other CEOs, respect them, and move them to change.
- These men and women are lifelong learners who enjoy solving problems.
- Their business networks of other CEOs, bankers, investors, vendors, and a wide variety of other significant resources will open doors. The chairmen of these groups have extraordinary networks of CEOs and service providers for middle-market firms.
- Through their experiences the members have learned how to work on the business and not just in it. They are strategic and operational thinkers that have built long-term value.
- They enjoy helping others succeed.

THE BOARD GROUP

This organization, founded by the authors, includes a select group of experienced CEOs and board members who serve on boards.

They assist middle market, privately-held companies in creating, organizing, and leading professional advisory boards. The purpose of the organization is to help business owners maximize sustainable value through better board processes. They develop professional board processes that can lead to consistently better decisions and excellent results. Their website is www.theboardgroup.com.

SELECTION MISTAKES TO AVOID

Avoid the following mistakes selecting board members who:

1. Make unilateral decisions. They are "tellers," not "listeners."

2. Are members only because they are friends of the owner or company insiders.

3. Are not willing to hold the CEO accountable to acting on board recommendations.

4. Lack strategic thinking ability.

5. Will tolerate meetings that do not allocate enough time to discuss and resolve critical issues.

6. Cannot foster alignment between shareholder interests and company results.

7. Are not respectful and collegial.

8. Are unable to commit to attending regular meetings.

9. Are unwilling to fully prepare for meetings.

10. Derive significant income from consulting with or providing professional advice to the company.

QUESTIONS AN ADVISORY BOARD CANDIDATE SHOULD ASK

Board candidates often ask, "What should I consider before accepting an invitation to join a board?" Outlined below are typical questions a potential board candidate may ask. As an owner, you need to be ready to answer questions like these:

Do the shareholders and CEO really want help? Is there unity on the decision to form a board?

How do you feel about the integrity of the shareholders and CEO? Are their value systems compatible with yours?

Is there transparency on the financials? Have you reviewed the outside CPA's prepared documents? Are they audited or reviewed?

Is it clear why the company wants me on their advisory board, and can I really help?

Who else has been selected to be on the board? Am I compatible in terms of experience and philosophy?

What are the legal ramifications? Are there any pending lawsuits or potential claims? Does the company have D&O Insurance and are they willing to indemnify the board? Is the balance sheet strong enough to support any legal filings against the company?

Does the company have a vision and a strategic plan that I can support?

How much time is required to be a 100 percent contributor?

Is the remuneration plan adequate for my time?

Is there a conflict of interest with other business relationships that I have?

RECOMMENDED PROCESS FOR FORMING AN ADVISORY BOARD

❖ Establish clear shareholder objectives for forming a board.

❖ Get clarity on the strategic intent of the shareholders and their commitment to building a company with sustainable value.

❖ Define the desired characteristics and experience of the advisory board.

❖ Define the search universe.

❖ Develop a sourcing and selection plan.

❖ Design an aligned evaluation process using the Criteria Scorecard.

❖ Retain experienced professionals to manage the process and make introductions if you need help.

REAL GAME, REAL BANK

IN MY 25 PLUS YEARS OF BANKING MID-SIZED COMPANIES, I HAVE BEEN INVOLVED WITH OVER 200 OF THE FINEST COMPANIES IN SOUTHERN CALIFORNIA. THE "BEST OF CLASS" COMPANIES HAVE COMMON CHARACTERISTICS... SUCH AS STRONG MANAGEMENT THAT RELIES ON OUTSIDE RESOURCES SUCH AS AN ADVISORY BOARD. CEO "ACCOUNTABILITY" COMBINED WITH THE AVAILABILITY OF VASTLY EXPANDED RESOURCES PROVIDED BY ADVISORY BOARD MEMBERS, YIELDS TOP TIER RESULTS!!

K. BRIAN HORTON, PRESIDENT AND DIRECTOR, 1ST ENTERPRISE BANK

The Advisory Board Wants to Know:

Consider the key decisions you need to make in the coming year. Whom would you want on a professional advisory board that would help you make those decisions and help you create sustainable value over the long term? Now, imagine a room of three to five experts who can give you the best information and advice so that you make great decisions.

1. What are the five key issues or opportunities that you need to consider?

2. What actions will have the greatest positive impact on the value of your company?

3. Considering your answers to 1 and 2 above, what experience do you need to bring into the room to ensure the best decisions?

4. What skills do you need to shape these decisions? Do you or your team have those skills?

5. Who would be the best people you know (or could imagine) that could help you make these decisions and take the needed actions?

6. How can you find and attract the people who will bring the skills and experience you need?

CHAPTER 4

Getting the Most Out of the Board

"Talent wins games, but teamwork and intelligence wins championships."
Michael Jordan

The board process will yield the greatest return on time, effort, and money when the owners, board members, and management work well together. As in any productive relationship, the players must commit to their roles and play their parts fully.

Governance Triangle

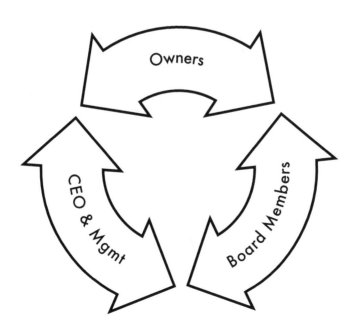

Each segment of this model consists of many components. In aggregate, when they function well, the three groups trust each other and hold each other accountable for their participation in a productive board process. The owner then gets the most out of his board and the process.

Some of the components of each leg of this Governance Diagram are:

- ❖ Clear definition of roles
- ❖ Defined and measured responsibilities
- ❖ Open, honest, and timely communication
- ❖ Actions that build value
- ❖ High level of alignment on direction, priorities, and culture

THE OWNER'S ROLE

In an interview on National Public Radio (NPR), retired US Army General Wesley Clark said, "The success of a campaign is determined by the clear vision of an outcome that is better than today."

The first step to getting the most success out of the board process is to decide what a "clear vision of an outcome that is better" looks like. How do the owners define success? The owners, the board, and the management team then can decide what game to play, how to play it, and how to keep score. This frames an efficient and effective board process that yields the most from the investment made in the board.

What Do Owners Want?

When company owners ask themselves, "What do we want from the business?" there are really two parts to the question:

- ❖ What outcome do the owners want personally from owning the business and when do they expect to achieve it?
- ❖ What does the business need to become so that it delivers the outcomes the owners want?

Owners should consider several outcomes. They can sell all of the company, sell a portion of the business, or keep the business as an investment that provides a competitive return on that investment. Chapter eight discusses these options in greater detail.

Define the Owners' Roles in the Board Process

Owners will get the most out of the board process by investing energy and time. Outlined below are actions owners can take that will help to ensure the board meets his or her expectations.

Have Clarity. The owners, as previously mentioned, must be clear on their objectives. Their objectives should be transparent and reviewed frequently with the board.

Establish Good Governance. Create and publish corporate governance principles so that all parties understand the rules under which the company is operating.

Be Accountable. The owners and CEO must be willing to be accountable to the board. A professional advisory board will demand it and real progress will only be made with that preamble.

Select the Best. Ensure that the best and most qualified persons are on the advisory board. Match skills and experience with the value drivers of the business.

Be Information Driven. Be transparent. Provide all the information requested. Let current data and metrics drive the decision making.

Meet Commitments. Debate the alternatives, but commit to a course of action. Taking action drives energy and motivation throughout the organization and fuels the board process.

Honor the Process. Keep the board meeting dates and ensure the meetings are conducted in a professional manner.

Consider a Non-Executive Chairman. Consider using an outside director to be non-executive chairman. He or she would facilitate the meeting, allowing the CEO and owners to listen and participate without concern about managing the meeting. (See Chapter Five for addition information.)

Set Agendas. Prepare the agenda for each meeting in collaboration with the non-executive chairman. Distribute the agenda along with the financial package well in advance of each scheduled meeting. Morning meetings are most productive and should be kept to five hours including lunch.

Define the Culture. Be sure the board understands the culture of the organization. What standards have been established? What are the values and philosophies that serve as guidelines both internally and externally? (See Chapter Six for more on board culture.)

Discuss Risk Tolerance. At the outset of a board's formation, the owners should make their tolerance for risk well-known and documented. Two risk areas often discussed are rate of growth and the amount of debt that owners will tolerate.

Present the Leadership Team. The board should have the opportunity to meet and evaluate the key management. Each functional leader should make presentations throughout the year.

Follow Up. Publish action initiatives at the completion of each meeting to facilitate communication and accountability.

Set Family Guidelines. Agree on the role of the owner's family members in the business and on how future family members will enter the business. Often, a family council of the owners is created to manage a family business. It will define the criteria a family member must meet to come into the business.

MANAGEMENT'S ROLE IN THE BOARD PROCESS

Management's role in an effective board process can be summarized as the creation of strategic and operational plans and execution of those plans. The outcomes are the strategic and financial results that the owners, board, and management agree on within the boundaries set by the owners and the board. These efforts are lead by the CEO who may or may not be an owner.

For a professional advisory board to properly advise a business, the board members need timely information from management in many areas. The communication areas are:

Planning

The owners and the board require several plans from management. The board's role is to understand the current and future implications of those plans, to challenge the assumptions and capabilities inherent in them, and to hold management accountable for executing these plans. The key plans are:

* Three-year strategic plan (strategic map)
* One-year tactical operating plan
* Overview of annual functional plans (marketing, operations, etc.)
* Ninety-day action plan
* CEO's top priorities
* Capital Expenditure plan (CapEx plan)

Financial Measures and Tracking

The core of the sustainable value model is financial performance. Management must provide timely, accurate, and consistent information in this area so that everyone can measure the financial performance of the company. Some of the financial reporting components are:

* Current and historical financial data
* Detailed financial analysis
* Key indicators (dashboard)
* Benchmarking with companies in similar SIC codes
* Bank term sheet
* Margin analysis by segment—products, customer offering, market, etc.
* Justification of any major investments based on ROI, operational need or competitive advantage

People and Organization

The strengths of each team member and the effectiveness of the organizational structure are the foundations of any business.

Management has the responsibility to present to the board its evaluation of its key players. It also should present the current and future organization chart of the team. The core reports are:

❖ Assessment of the leadership team

❖ Organizational structure both current and future

❖ Key actions to attract, retain, and train game-breaking talent

❖ Management development and succession planning

Technology

Technological changes and challenges continue to accelerate. Managing the impact of these changes has become a priority for all companies. The board needs to understand management's plan for keeping the company current and competitive. The board will ask for:

❖ Technology assessments—review of patents and intellectual property

❖ Technology plan and the investments needed for operational efficiency and effectiveness

❖ Technology road map for competitive advantage

Management Systems

Businesses run on their systems and processes. The better the systems are documented, understood, and followed, the more efficient and effective the company. If boards understand how the systems work, they can create significant breakthroughs by leading the discussion in systems theory and systems thinking. In the words of the old Ma Bell ads, "The system is the solution."

Companies without good discipline and systems tend to blame individuals for errors or problems. When professional boards see this culture, they will ask, "What was the system that managed this area and what part of the system did not work?" A much later question is, "Who was responsible?"

Key Indicators

The dashboard of key performance indicators (KPIs) may vary widely by industry and company life cycle. The board, the owners, and the management team must agree on what to measure and report on a timely basis. Some of these key indicators look in the past, others are current, and some look forward. If the board and management team can quickly see where they have been, where they are currently, and where they are headed, they are more likely to consistently make good decisions.

Legal and Risk Management

The first rule in this area is no surprises. All companies operate in a treacherous legal environment. Suits or bad legal commitments can destroy companies. PABoards and management help to ensure that the company has protection through processes that are legal, consistent, and well documented. Management is responsible for all significant legal commitments but reviews them with the board prior to action.

Management's Monthly Board Reporting Template

The following is a recommended format for the monthly financial report to the board:

1. Executive Summary (good, bad, and ugly)

2. Profit and Loss (actual, budget, prior year, comparative)

3. Balance Sheet

4. Cash Flow

5. Key Financial Indicators (trended over time)

REAL GAME, REAL PEOPLE

OUR COMPANY BUILT OUR ADVISORY BOARD OVER TEN YEARS AGO. WHILE THE COMPANY WAS ON A GOOD GROWTH TRAJECTORY, IT BECAME APPARENT TO ME THAT WE WERE GOING TO OUTGROW OUR PEOPLE, MONEY SUPPLY, AND SYSTEMS. OUR SOLUTION WAS TO BRING IN OUTSIDERS WITH SKILLS IN AREAS THAT WE WERE LACKING IN OUR OWNERSHIP OR MANAGEMENT TEAM.

THE BOARD BROUGHT EXTERNAL PERSPECTIVE AND SEASONED JUDGMENT THAT HELPED THE OWNERSHIP AND EXECUTIVE MANAGEMENT DEVELOP A CLEAR UNDERSTANDING OF THE OWNERSHIP GOALS AND A FRAMEWORK TO BUILD SUSTAINABLE VALUE. ONCE OWNERSHIP, MANAGEMENT, AND THE ADVISORY BOARD WERE ALL IN SYNC, THE BOARD HELPED US DEVELOP FOCUS ON THE CRITICAL ISSUES. IT PROVIDED REAL DIRECTION TO GROW PAST MANY OF THE OBSTACLES WE FACED ALONG THE WAY.

LAST, BUT NOT LEAST, WE DEVELOPED AN IMPROVED REPORTING PROCESS THAT BROUGHT HEIGHTENED VISIBILITY AND INCREASED GOVERNANCE TO OUR TEAM. TOGETHER, THE BOARD, OWNERSHIP, AND OUR MANAGEMENT TEAM, DESIGNED A NEW BUSINESS MODEL WITH SEVERAL INNOVATIONS THAT HAS HELPED INCREASE OUR SHAREHOLDER VALUE TODAY

ALLAN KECK, CEO, R.W. SMITH COMPANY, SAN DIEGO, CA

CEO's BOARD ROLE

The CEO, whether he or she is the owner or a person hired for the role, is responsible for all aspects of the company and its performance. The management actions mentioned earlier are conducted under the leadership of the CEO. If he is not the owner, he must learn to work with the board to gain their trust and support so that he can carry out his plans.

BOARD MEMBERS' ROLES

Winning can be defined as exceeding expectations. Here are ways to ensure that the board members understand and meet the owners' expectations. The next chapter discusses several of these in more detail.

Charter. The advisory board charter is the document that provides board members with their rules of engagement and the owners' expectations of the board.

Board Culture. If the board charter is the "why" of the board process, then the board culture defines the "how." It is the board's style. That style may change with the needs of the company, but the fundamental question is whether the board's role is primarily oversight of management or if it is collaboration with and support of management. Oversight cultures might use words, such as challenge, discovery, driver, control, requirements, and authority. Collaborative cultures might be defined by support, collaborate, encourage, coaching, and openness. The goal of both cultural styles is to create a profitable, productive, valuable company led by a trusted, motivated, and competent management team.

Another part of board culture is how board members work together. Some components of working together are asking great questions; listening; respectful challenge; care for the owners, the company, and management; and thorough preparation.

Board Calendar. The calendar outlines meeting dates, themes for the meetings, and other company events that may be pertinent to the board. Commit to twelve months of meeting dates.

Evaluations. The advisory board must create a process to evaluate the business, management, the CEO, and itself. There is value in the truism: "What gets measured gets managed, and what gets managed gets improved." The board expects the owner and management to create the plans for winning and an appropriate instrument panel that selects both key financial and operating indicators of performance. The board holds the CEO and management accountable for achieving the agreed upon plans. The non-executive chairman and the owners need to agree on how to evaluate the performance of the individual board members. Some criteria for evaluations are attendance, preparation, participation, contributions, and impact.

Commitment. Owners want commitment from their advisory board members to stay engaged and regularly attend scheduled meetings. Advisory boards also want commitment from the owners and CEO. Board members want to know the owners and CEO are professional, deeply involved and commited to improving the value of the business.

Availability. Advisory board members expect the controlling shareholder and CEO to be available to discuss the monthly information and to deal with issues on a timely basis. The CEO expects the same from the board members.

Term Limits. Outline term limits for board members in the advisory board charter. The infusion of new perspectives, ideas, and energy is important to avoid stagnation and to encourage the business to successfully evolve. Board term limits also help to diminish the concentration of influence in a small number of individuals and to weed out inactive or difficult advisory board members.

Executive Session. Highly functioning advisory boards have an executive session at the close of each meeting to discuss, without management. In this session, the board members can discuss critical concerns that may be difficult, confidential, or inappropriate to discuss during the board meeting.

Non-Executive Chairman Communication. It is important that the CEO, the chairman, and the non-executive chairman discuss the board meeting agenda before the board meetings. After the meeting, they should review the pertinent action initiatives. The non-executive chairman is responsible for following up with the CEO between meetings.

Committee Reports. In many cases, the advisory board will appoint an audit and/or compensation committee. Their reports should be included on the board agenda, and the committee chairman should have open access to management.

Rhythm. A board, over time, develops into a team, and the process advances to a highly performing rhythm. Do not disturb the rhythm by canceling meetings or letting the meeting drift into the weeds.

RED FLAGS FOR PROBLEMS IN THE BOARD PROCESS

The members of the board, management, and the owners should be aware of how well the board process is operating. This performance evaluation is judged against the board charter and the progress the company is making toward creating sustainable value. If any participant is not performing his or her role well, the behavior creates a "red flag." Distill these red flags into a one-page document. The process of discussing and defining the red flags gives the board a common language for holding itself accountable for high performance.

PABoard Process Red Flags

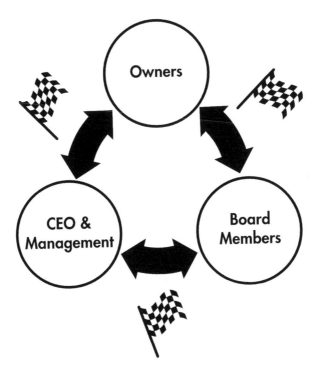

Red flags for board members' performance:

1. Not attending meetings regularly
2. Not doing homework (not reading the information in the board-meeting package)
3. Not participating in the meeting discussions
4. Not being available between meetings
5. Failure to show respect for the other board members or management
6. Not listening to or understanding the owner's needs
7. Too much involvement in operating detail
8. Being overbearing or showing disruptive behavior during board meetings

Red flags for management's performance:

1. Weak strategic thinking and planning
2. Poor results against planned objectives
3. Lack of preparation of relevant information on the discussion issues
4. Frequent rescheduling of meeting dates
5. Not following through on actions agreed to in board meetings
6. Lack of participation and involvement in the meetings
7. Unwillingness to fully discuss critical issues
8. Providing only one solution and no evaluation of alternatives

Red flags for the chairman's performance:

1. Not allocating enough time in the agenda to critical issues
2. Not preparing an agenda

3. Not preparing the CEO properly for a meeting

4. Not keeping the meeting discussions at an appropriate strategic level

Red flags for owner's performance:

1. Not providing clear definitions of the outcomes he or she wants

2. Being unclear about values and business principles

3. Not supporting the decisions of the board

4. Including too many insiders or family members on the board

5. Bringing family issues to the board meetings

FINANCIAL INVESTMENT IN THE PABOARD PROCESS

For a public company, the compensation for the board of directors is typically handled through board fees and company stock. The options are more flexible for a privately-held company with a professional advisory board. Here are the financial investments to consider:

1. **Compensation.** Remember the old saying "You can't get something for nothing"? Properly compensate advisory board members because if you pay for the advice, you are more likely to follow it. Proper compensation also shows respect for the board members' time, expertise and impact. The board members also appreciate the respect and the owner's commitment associated with the compensation. Here are several forms of compensation:

   ❖ Annual retainer

   ❖ Payment of fees for each board session attended

   ❖ Fees for committee meetings

   ❖ Phantom stock or value participation rights

   ❖ Share in ultimate exit value

   ❖ Stock options or warrants

2. **Costs per Quarter.** Generally, advisory board members receive a stipend for attending the meeting. Budget this payment on a quarterly basis. Financial compensation can range from $2,500 per meeting to $10,000 per quarter (part retainer, part meeting fee). Many companies choose to compensate advisory board members with a mix of cash and equity participation.

3. **Retainer.** Some companies use a combination of annual retainer and per-meeting fee. These retainers can range between $10,000 and $35,000 per year. The retainer covers phone calls, meetings, and issue-oriented meetings they attend between formal board meetings.

4. **Value Participation.** The size of the value participation should be large enough to be an incentive to advisory board members and make them feel they have a stake in the future value of the company. Determining the right metrics to measure performance is challenging but essential. Paying with company stock or granting stock options is a good way to bind the interests of the board members to the interests of the company. For privately held companies, "phantom stock," some form of "value participation rights," or a cash payout may create compensation if there is a change of control of ownership. Stock options can be issued on an annual basis. These are ways to compensate board members (and management) with financial rewards tied to the performance of the company.

5. **Other Costs.** Paying for lodging and travel is customary as well. If the company recruits locally for board members, this can reduce travel expenses; however, a company should not restrict itself geographically if the needed talent is outside of the area.

6. **Insurance.** For a formal board of directors, a Directors and Officers (D&O) policy is recommended.. For advisory boards, have an attorney prepare a memo of understanding for the board and a letter of indemnification.

REASONS WHY ADVISORY BOARDS FAIL TO DELIVER VALUE

If you as a shareholder or owner do not manage your part of the board process, the outcomes will not meet your expectations. If the board members are not delivering an energetic, effective process then the process will fail. Use the Governance Triangle model and the red flags to diagnose the areas for improvement. Here are some other reasons that advisory boards fail:

1. Lack of reliable, consistent, and timely operating and strategic information, leading to nonproductive meetings and uninformed decisions

2. Owners and CEO not committed to the board process or to implementing board suggestions

3. Lack of strategic focus

4. Too much meeting time spent on reporting and not enough time for addressing critical issues

5. Misalignment among the owners, CEO, management, and the board

6. Board members not respectful

7. Infrequent, irregular board meetings

8. Experience and skills of the board members not matching the strategic drivers or threats to the business

9. Management not prepared for meetings

PROFESSIONAL ADVISORY BOARD PROCESS EVALUATION

Appendix A contains a checklist for evaluating the disciplines and systems of a professional advisory board process. The higher the score, the more likely the company is building Exceptional Sustainable Value. Score your current process and look for areas for improvement.

The Advisory Board Wants to Know:

PABoard members will ask the CEO some challenging questions. They may want to know if the CEO respects the board process. Will he value the advice and judgment the board members bring and act on it? In order for an advisory board to become a competitive asset, everyone involved must contribute information, thought, respectful challenge, and caring. The board will want to know:

1. What do the owners want? What are their biggest fears and issues? What is most valuable to them?

2. What do the owners want from a board process? How will they measure the value from their investment in the board?

3. Are the owners willing to invest the personal time, staff time, money, and the openness to get the full value from the board process?

4. Will the owners and the CEO follow up, change, and act on the decisions made in the meetings?

5. Are the owners willing to build alignment between the board and management by giving them long-term equity incentives?

6. Are the board members performing at a high level? How will they measure their performance?

7. Is management contributing to a highly performing board process? How do you measure them?

CHAPTER 5

The Chairman's Playbook

*"Freedom is the greatest when rules of behavior
are clear and enforced."*
Plato

The board, like the company, needs to manage itself so that it executes efficiently, effectively, and consistently. It must have a process that moves the company from entrepreneurial towards more professional governance. The leader of the process is either the chairman of the board or the non-executive chairman.

The Chairman's Playbook is a useful tool for guiding the PABoard process. The five-part structure keeps meetings focused and generates the dialogue that moves the company towards its end game.

The organizational document and legal instrument sections provide guidelines as to how proper corporate governance practices are instituted and reviewed.

The management section prepares corporate executives to communicate with the board and focus on critical issues.

NON-EXECUTIVE CHAIRMAN

A professional advisory board is most effective when led by a non-executive chairman. A non-executive chair normally works with the CEO to establish the agenda, keep the meeting focused on strategic issues and key initiatives and ensure accountability for agreed upon actions.

A non-executive chairman ensures that the documents described in this chapter are created. The process of creating them helps ensure professional governance and processes in the company.

The chairman should be experienced in managing the board process. This person should be task driven, good at creating structure and process, and possess leadership skills that lead to well run meetings. Finally, the chair must model and manage accountability for the board and the CEO.

REAL GAME, REAL PEOPLE
PHIL MATTHEWS, FORMER CHAIRMAN OF WOLVERINE PRODUCTS AND SIZZLER RESTAURANTS AND CURRENT CHAIRMAN OF ZODIAC MARINE PRODUCTS

NON-EXECUTIVE CHAIRMAN ROLE

MUCH HAS BEEN WRITTEN ABOUT THE ROLE OF BOARD LEADERSHIP IN CREATING SHAREHOLDER VALUE, BUT NOTHING COMPARES TO THE IMPACT OF THE CHAIRMAN AND THE ROLE ASSUMED BY THIS LEADER. THIS STARRING ROLE CAN BE DEFINED AND ACTED OUT IN NUMEROUS WAYS—BOTH POSITIVELY AND NEGATIVELY. LET'S FIRST EXAMINE THE TYPE OF CHAIRMAN ROLES AVAILABLE TO A CHAIR, AND THE DIFFERENCES OF EACH.

THERE ARE BASICALLY TWO TYPES OF CHAIRS—THOSE FOCUSING ON GOVERNANCE AND THOSE FOCUSING ON ADVANCING THE BUSINESS. THE GOVERNANCE MODEL SETS THE CHAIR'S PRIORITIES AS MANAGING THE BOARD MEETINGS, SETTING THE BOARD'S AGENDA TO PROTECT GOOD GOVERNANCE, ENSURING THE VARIOUS COMMITTEES ARE FUNCTIONING PROPERLY, AND ASSESSING THE PERFORMANCE OF THE COMPANY AND ITS LEADERS.

THE BUSINESS MODEL SETS THE CHAIR'S PRIORITIES AS FACILITATING THE MEETINGS, SETTING THE AGENDA AGAINST THE BUSINESS NEEDS, WORKING WITH MANAGEMENT TO MAKE SURE COMMITTEES ARE SUPPORTIVE OF BUSINESS REQUIREMENTS, AND ASSESSING THE PERFORMANCE OF THE COMPANY AND ITS LEADERS.

IN BOTH, PERFORMANCE IS ASSESSED, BUT THE LATTER MODEL CONFERS A MORE COLLABORATIVE ENVIRONMENT ON THE BOARD, AND THE CHAIR IS GENERALLY VIEWED MORE AS AN ADVISOR.

WHILE MANY WOULD SAY THE REAL ROAD TO CHAIRMAN EXCELLENCE IS TO FIND A BALANCE BETWEEN THE TWO, IT IS SELDOM ACHIEVABLE GIVEN THE PERSONALITIES, COMPANY SITUATIONS, AND NEEDS OF THE BUSINESS. MOST CHAIRS END UP LEANING ONE WAY OR THE OTHER. THEREFORE, IT IS MY STRONG RECOMMENDATION TO THOSE TAKING ON THESE NON-EXECUTIVE CHAIRMAN ROLES THAT THEY DECIDE UP FRONT WHICH OF THE TWO ROLES IS BEST FOR THEM AND THE COMPANY.

CHAIRMAN'S PLAYBOOK STRUCTURE

Governance is made more effective and efficient by following a playbook developed by the authors that includes five sections:

1. Board Process and Structure

2. Company Organizational Documents

3. *Legal Instruments*

4. *Management Preparation*

5. *Board Meeting Agenda*

It illustrates the information that should be available for the board meetings and which should have been reviewed by the non-executive chair and board members. These playbook documents will be developed as the PABoard process evolves.

SECTION 1: BOARD PROCESS AND STRUCTURE

Chairman's role

The chairman is responsible for the board process and its outcomes. He manages the agenda by ensuring that the important issues are on the agenda, in the right order, and with adequate time allowed for discussion. If he has not delegated the board meeting facilitation to his non-executive chair, he manages the board meeting so that the board stays focused and conducts itself appropriately with each other and management. He is the keeper of the corporate culture. The CEO reports to the chairman. The chairman often with the advice from a Compensation Committee, recommends the CEO's compensation, and the board approves it. The chairman often has the power to appoint board members.

Board Charter

A charter explains the mission of the board. It explains why the shareholders created the board, the expectations the shareholders have of the advisors, and the advisor's expectations of management. It spells out details of the formation of the advisory board, such as size and membership composition. Other sections deal with board member evaluations, committee compensation, confidentiality, solicitation, conflicts of interest, and unfair competition. See Appendix B for examples of board charters.

Board Calendars

Part of the value of the board process is the regular focus on the critical aspects of the company and its management. By institutionalizing this process into an annual board calendar, the shareholders and management must be prepared to address, on a scheduled basis, the professionalization of the company and the pursuit of value creation.

The annual board calendar should have quarterly meetings with specific governance themes:

❖ *People evaluations, succession planning, and organizational structure*

❖ *Key issues progress*

❖ *Strategic plan review*

❖ *Annual operational plan and budget performance reviews*

Board Composition

The Chairman's Playbook should include the biographical information on each advisory board member as well as all contact information.

CEO Authority

The board should develop—with the chairman—the levels of authority that the CEO has so that there are no surprises in the management of the company. Authority levels should be set for spending according to budget commitments, capital expenditures budgets, and non-budget items. The board and the CEO should agree on the oversight the board will require in areas of hiring and firing of direct reports to the CEO, company policies, employee benefits, and lease commitments and other contracts. The CEO should understand what he can commit to without prior board consultation.

Committees

Professional advisory boards may have an audit and a compensation committee. Each committee, depending on the size of the board, will have a chairman and a separate charter.

Audit Committee. The audit committee chairman is responsible for coordinating with the CPA firm on audits or reviews. They review the profit and loss and balance sheet statements. They also make recommendations to the owners on the reliability of the financial statements and the process for preparing them.

Compensation Committee. The compensation committee chairman is responsible for recommending CEO and executive compensation plans. The compensation committee is also responsible for recommending board compensation to include meeting fees, consulting arrangements, and change of control agreements.

Nomination Committee. The non-executive chair is usually responsible for the nomination committee's functions: evaluating board member performance, removing non-performers, and identifying new member candidates.

Committee of the Whole. Many smaller companies do not use governance committees. They use the advisory board as a "committee of the whole," which means they bring audit, compensation, and board performance issues before the entire board. These companies may create ad hoc committees to focus on specific issues such as strategic planning or acquisitions.

Section 2: Company Organizational Documents

Code of Ethics

A company needs certain written policies to guide employees with respect to standards of conduct. The document should spell out improper activities that could damage the company's reputation and otherwise result in serious adverse consequences. If a company is conducting business internationally, a PABoard will coach management to review and comply with all facets of the Federal Corrupt Practices Act.

Corporate Governance Communication

Since PABoards deal with non-public companies, the corporate governance guidelines are directed at ensuring the organization adheres to certain principles:

❖ Create and publish corporate governance principles so that employees and others can understand the company's operational guidelines.

❖ Provide employees with an internal mechanism to alert management and the advisory board of potential misconduct issues.

❖ Ensure prompt disclosure of any significant material issues or developments.

❖ Establish a compensation structure that directly links management to the interests and end game of the owner and shareholders.

Disaster/Crisis Plan

Business continuity planning requires a company to have a written plan of action for response to a natural disaster or a reputation crisis that could threaten the business. Disaster and crisis situations can include accidents, fire, flood, earthquakes, legal disputes, theft, or a situation that threatens the integrity or reputation of the company. The goal is to be able to manage a crisis well so that the company can continue operations, the employees and customers are safe, and damage can be minimized.

Develop a crisis plan—uncomfortable but necessary—to manage through the death of the owner and/or CEO. The plan may include converting an advisory board to a fiduciary board with clear instructions on selling or holding the business for the remaining family or shareholders.

Compensation Plan

An ideal compensation plan motivates employees, ensures pay equity, and controls salary costs, but compensation includes many aspects beyond straight salary. A well-designed compensation plan includes benefits, time off, stock options, and the extras that employees view as valuable. Compensation is a balancing act. Pay too much and there is a drain on company resources. Pay too little and the company will find it hard to compete to attract and retain a quality workforce. Measure compensation levels against performance, against other employees in the company, and against employees in comparable positions at other companies. Market factors play a part, and the compensation plan needs to consider prevailing wages and salaries for its industry and locale.

The most challenging and impactful compensation plan for the board is the CEO's compensation. Every plan is different because it must fit the CEO, the company's issues and opportunities, methods of measurement, level of total compensation relative to the company's ability to pay, the owner's values, desired outcomes, and many other factors.

If the CEO is a hired professional who is not the owner, the compensation plan will be different from one for the CEO who is the owner. That CEO's plan will focus on EBITDA growth and value building. If the CEO is the owner, his primary decision on his compensation is how much he wants to take out of the business vs. leave in the business to invest in growth.

Here are general guidelines for CEO compensation when the CEO is not the owner:

1. Be heavily weighted on achieving financial success in the short and long term.

2. Have components related to achieving non-financial parts of the strategic plan, such as customer and product diversification, customer satisfaction, corporate culture and ethics, and quality of management team.

3. Be competitive with the market price for a CEO of this size company in this particular industry.

4. Include equity ownership or value participation in the value that the CEO commits to create in the strategic plan.

5. Be built around mutually agreed upon measures of success.

6. Have short-term bonus opportunities for reaching annual financial goals.

Organizational Plan

Management should prepare an organization chart reflecting the executive level positions along with the reporting relationships three levels below the CEO.

A succession plan should be an annually updated addendum. It should show the key people in the organization, their potential for growth, and their contribution. It may also delineate development plans for each. This plan should be a significant part of the board calendar with at least one session a year devoted to organizational and personal growth.

Safety Plan

Playing it safe is just good business. Insurance companies contend that a business' safety plan is an easy and effective way to save money while protecting employees. Federal OSHA regulations require a safety document from many companies. About half of the states require almost all companies to have a written safety plan. In California, for example, state law requires every company with more than ten workers to have a written job safety program. Components include developing safety procedures, appointing a safety committee, performing ongoing inspections, and safety training. Many safety programs can be built using resources available from casualty insurance companies and other state or federal agencies.

SECTION 3: LEGAL INSTRUMENTS

Buy/Sell Agreement

A buyout agreement, typically referred to as a buy/sell agreement, is a binding contract between shareholders of a business. It dictates what will happen if a shareholder dies or must otherwise leave the business. Sometimes called a "business will," it is also likened to a premarital agreement between business partners and shareholders. Life insurance policies are often used to fund the agreement when a shareholder's death triggers the buy/sell agreement. "Surviving shareholders generally want to ensure a continuity of ownership and management without having the departing shareholder's successor thrust upon them," says Howard Davidoff, CPA, a professor at the City University of New York, in an article for The CPA Journal, publication of the New York State Society of CPAs. "Nor do they want to unduly compromise the liquidity needs of the business by funding a significant buyout; disabled or deceased shareholders would want their families compensated fairly for their share of the business. A properly drafted buy/sell agreement can achieve all of these goals."

Bylaws

Circulate the corporate bylaws to all the advisory board members for review of the statutory provisions and reevaluate annually.

D&O Insurance

Directors and Officers liability (D&O) insurance can provide financial protection for fiduciary and advisory board members and officers of the corporation in the event of a lawsuit because of actions they took in service to the company. Some liken it to Errors and Omissions liability (E&O) insurance for management and the board. While D&O insurance is often confused with E&O insurance, the two are not synonymous. E&O insurance covers performance failures and negligence while D&O covers the performance and duties of management. D&O insurance covers damages or defense costs that result from a lawsuit for alleged wrongful acts. Coverage can extend to defense costs arising out of criminal and regulatory investigations in addition to civil actions. Most underwriters will add advisory board members to the D&O policy without an increase in premium.

Indemnification Agreement

The authors recommend that the company provide indemnification agreements for the advisory board members that provide first dollar coverage to augment the D&O insurance. This agreement defines when and how the company will defend its board of advisors if they and the company are sued. It is also important to remember that the indemnification agreement is only as good as the company's balance sheet. Potential new board members should have their attorney review this document to understand its coverage and terms.

Non-Compete Agreement

Sometimes controversial, non-compete agreements are contracts between an employer and an employee in which employees promise not to take what they learn at a company and then use it while working for a competitor. Typically, these agreements say the employee shall not work for rivals, try to recruit current clients, or otherwise compete for a specified period of time after leaving the company. Because general agreements signed by all employees tend not to hold up in court, many companies opt for non-compete agreements written for key employees. This is an important area in which to seek legal advice.

Intellectual Property Agreement

Key employees should sign an intellectual property (IP) agreement that defines the company's IP, the employee's relationship to existing IP, and to IP that an employee develops.

Non-Disclosure Agreement

Advisory board members and key employees should sign a non-disclosure agreement (NDA). Also known as a confidentiality agreement, the NDA is a legal contract between two parties that outlines confidential information that will be shared with the board, but must not be shared with third parties. The NDA creates a confidential relationship between the parties to protect proprietary information and trade secrets, the type of information not accessible to the general public. These are useful tools when companies and individuals are considering doing business together and need to better understand what is going on before they make a final decision to move forward. Some employee agreements include an NDA clause. To create a proper NDA, seek competent legal advice.

Shareholder Agreement

A shareholder agreement is a contract between a company and its shareholders, which details how the firm will be managed, how internal differences will be resolved, and what will happen if a shareholder dies, resigns, is terminated, becomes incapacitated, or even goes bankrupt. The best time to deal with "what if" scenarios is before they happen. A typical shareholder agreement will include:

1. Who can be a shareholder?

2. Who can serve on the board of directors?

3. What happens if a shareholder dies or becomes disabled?

4. What is the valuation methodology to determine the value of the shares of stock?

5. Is the corporation required to buy the shares of a shareholder who is leaving?

6. How will shareholders be paid if they sell their shares?

Minutes and Legal Filings of the Fiduciary Board

The advisory board should be apprised of resolutions and legal actions taken by the fiduciary board.

SECTION 4: MANAGEMENT PREPARATION

Annual Operating Plan

This plan is the document that management submits to the board each year. It contains several key components:

1. Annual key objectives, both financial and non-financial
2. Actions that management will take to reach these objectives
3. Customer, product, and system goals
4. Investment opportunities and costs
5. Organizational chart changes and development plans for staff members
6. KPIs to track key indicators of current and future business performance

Annual Financial Budget

This is the financial projection and commitment by the management team to the owners and the board. It includes the projected profit and loss statement, the balance sheet, cash flow projections, and the capital investment requirements for the fiscal year.

Auditor's Management Letter

The company's auditors prepare this document annually. It addresses financial issues and those operational issues within the scope of the audit. The board should ensure that management addresses the issues raised.

Capital Expenditure Budget

The projected investments to be made quarterly should be sent to the advisory board along with calculations on intended rate of returns. Investments in this budget usually have payouts greater than one year.

Credit Agreement

Review the bank credit agreement and covenant adherence quarterly. This agreement may create significant constraints on the company and its owners. It may require personal guarantees by the owners and limit their compensation. It will specify the financial ratios that you must maintain in order for the company to keep its credit lines and loans with the bank.

Financial Contingency Plan

The time to develop a financial contingency plan is before the business needs it. There will always be situations beyond the control of management that impact cash flow. These might include interest rate hikes, labor strikes, or natural disasters. A business can survive a period of limited sales or profits, but it cannot survive without cash to pay its obligations. A primary component of a financial contingency plan is management's plan to deal with business slowdown and its impact on the company's operations. When the slump occurs, the company must be prepared to take corrective action.

Key Performance Indicators and Dashboard

Similar to the operating plan, it is important to include in the financial presentation the key financial indicators and a dashboard. Key indicators measure progress, and when plotted over time, demonstrate at a glance, how well different aspects of a business are performing. They also project how well the company should perform in the future. The dashboard of key indicators is often shown in table form and supplemented with graphical presentations so that trends are visible. See an example in Appendix D.

While not an exhaustive list, the following financial reporting categories are recommended:

1. Liquidity ratios
2. Working capital ratios
3. Balance sheet leverage
4. Debt coverage and bank covenants
5. Profitability
6. Growth
7. Sustainability
8. Efficiency

Strategic Plan

The chairman and board members should have a copy of the strategic plan. This is the document that the management team has created and committed to deliver. It is the primary, long-term guidance for short-term tactics. It includes the company's mission, vision of the future, and plans to deliver both. If it is executed well, it will produce sustainable value. Without it, the company has no operating focus, and the board has no way to hold the team accountable for its actions or reward it for performance. More detail on this critical document and process are shown in Chapter Six. Also, Appendix C shows the central questions that shape the preparation of a strategic plan.

Ninety-Day Plans

Following each quarterly meeting, the board and the CEO need to define what will happen before the next quarterly board meeting. This Ninety-Day Plan process is an excellent device for ensuring that there is commitment to follow through between meetings. The follow-through creates value, which is the primary goal of the board. Without these short-term action plans, the meetings only generate hope for change.

Vision

Vision is defined as a picture of the company three years from the date of the strategic planning session. It describes where the company will arrive if it is successful. The CEO should lead with this document as his "north star." If the employees and board see this picture as compelling, real, tangible, achievable, and beneficial to them, then they will commit to that future. With a clear understanding of the vision, the team can create a strategic plan to reach it.

Section 5: Board Meeting Agenda

PABoard meetings usually last four to six hours. Send the agenda, financial reports, key indicator dashboards, and related material to the members at least three days prior to the meeting. It is recommended to have a conference call a few days prior to the actual board meeting to discuss the financial information to allow more time at the board meeting to discuss and explore issues on the agenda.

It is recommended that the meetings be chaired by a non-executive chairman who is experienced in managing the process. This ensures an efficient and effective meeting and allows the CEO and the other members to participate fully in the meeting.

Agenda Format

Call to Order. Chairman or non-executive chairman calls the meeting to order.

Opening Remarks by CEO. The CEO gives a highlights report, which is an overview on what has happened since the last meeting and relates the current top issues that he and the team are dealing with.

Review Minutes or Action Items from Last Meeting. Start meetings by refreshing everyone's memory of what was decided at the previous meeting and report of actions taken.

Financial Report. CFO or controller presents the current and projected profit and loss statements, balance sheet, and any other key financial information at a level of detail that satisfies the board. It should lead to understanding the issues and critical details, but it is not so detailed that it satisfies the needs of a CPA or family members who are very detailed. Too much detail bogs down a meeting and deflects the discussion from critical issues. Make backup detail available as requested.

Ninety-Day Action Review. This is a review of the actions that were committed to in the last board meeting. This follow through drives accountability and progress.

Committee Reports. If there are too many issues or some issues are just too complex for the entire board to handle, the board should form special committees. These committees will meet quarterly or when critical issues need to be discussed. If a committee has met since the last advisory board meeting, then the chairperson of that committee should present a report to the board.

Critical Organizational Functions. This is the time to review the status of strategic objectives, capital projects, industry trends, competitive intelligence, personnel and structural changes, and IT initiatives.

Key Issues. As a board learns to work together and trust builds, the board level views of reporting speed up. This allows time for substantive discussion of important issues. There must be openness, respect, and challenge. Key decisions are fully vetted. This is what most shareholders and operators want from the advisory board: good recommendations and suggested actions on tough, complex questions.

Preliminary Agenda for Next Meeting. The advisory board, the CEO, and the chairman will determine the vital issues to be addressed at the next meeting. Confirm the next four meeting dates.

Meeting Recap. Board members and management each recap the key points of the meeting to ensure the most important decisions and actions are not lost in the volume of ideas in the meeting. A ninety-day action plan is agreed to. The CEO and the board members also critique the board meeting process looking for constant improvement.

Executive Session. The board members should meet at the end of the meeting without the CEO or other management in the room. This time becomes particularly important if there are critical issues that involve the CEO's performance or ownership issues.

REAL GAME, REAL PEOPLE

THOMAS NIELSEN, FORMER VICE CHAIRMAN OF THE IRVINE COMPANY HAS THESE THOUGHTS ABOUT THE USE OF A CHAIRMAN'S PLAYBOOK

THE CHAIRMAN'S PLAYBOOK IS A MEANINGFUL AND ESSENTIAL TOOL IN BRINGING PROCESS AND RESULTS TO A PROFESSIONAL ADVISORY BOARD.

EXPERIENCE GAINED THROUGH NUMEROUS BOARD MEETINGS CONFIRMS THAT ADHERING TO THE BOARD PROCESS AND STRUCTURE KEEPS THE MEETINGS FOCUSED ON THE KEY ISSUES. IT GENERATES A LEVEL OF DIALOGUE THAT RESULTS IN MEANINGFUL STRATEGIC INITIATIVES, CLARITY, AND EXPECTATIONS THAT WILL DRIVE THE COMPANY TOWARD A MONETIZING EVENT.

THE ORGANIZATIONAL DOCUMENT AND LEGAL INSTRUMENT SECTIONS PROVIDE THE BOARD WITH GUIDELINES TO ENSURE THAT CORPORATE GOVERNANCE IS PROPERLY INSTITUTED AND FREQUENTLY REVIEWED.

THE MANAGEMENT PREPARATION SECTION PROVIDES A PRACTICAL FORMAT FOR USE BY THE COMPANY EXECUTIVES TO COMMUNICATE WITH THE BOARD AND SINGLE OUT CRITICAL COMPANY ISSUES.

FINALLY, ADHERING TO THE BOARD MEETING PROCESS SECTION RESULTS IN MEANINGFUL, PRODUCTIVE MEETINGS OF THE BOARD.

Ready for the Game

Successful leaders know that winning is based on solid preparation and strong teams. The past chapters have defined the issues, structures, and actions you need to create a solid board and business foundation for overcoming the Five Challenges, changing the game to more professional processes and building sustainable value. Appendix E is a summary checklist for the parts of the Chairman's Playbook.

The Advisory Board Wants to Know:

Experienced advisory board chairmen of privately-held companies will want to know if the business has its governance house in order and if it is regularly updated. Chairmen will ask many questions related to each of the sections in this chapter and here are a few key questions:

1. Are buy/sell agreements in place?

2. What are the strategic, annual operating, and budget plans, and how is the company doing compared to those plans?

3. Is the company operating well within bank loan covenant restrictions?

4. What are the key indicators of success and how are they trending?

5. What is the organizational structure and what is the succession plan?

6. What are the company's compensation philosophy and the CEO's compensation plan? Do they align with the value builders in the strategic plan?

7. Does the company have D&O insurance and are the directors covered?

Part III:

Leveraging Advisors to Build Sustainable Value

CHAPTER 6

Management's Playbook

"You can't cheat the game. You have to be prepared."
Mike Krzyzewski,
Duke University Basketball Head Coach

What if you were asked today, "How well are you and your team running your company?" How would you answer? You might say, "Really well. We are ahead of all our projections." Or you might answer evasively, "It depends on how you measure it." With either answer, you would want to put your answer in some sort of performance context. What outcomes are desirable? How soon? What profits are expected? What risks do we take? What is the scorecard? How are we doing compared to the competition?

All these questions and more are used by the board to help the owners, management, and the board agree on the game being played, how to keep score, and how well the organization is playing it. When all participants reach this agreement, there is strategic and operational alignment. With alignment, the organization can focus its resources and actions. The company can move efficiently toward its goals.

As actions are taken and results are achieved, the team gains energy and belief in itself. Trust develops in the plan, in the leadership, and in the rewards that will accrue to the team and the owners. The organization moves into "the zone," where it plays the game at its highest level and is better than the competition. And, the CEO can answer the question, "How well are you playing the game?" with a strong, "We play like real professionals, and here is how we know we are winning."

Here are the seven fundamentals to playing like a professional:

1. Define success.

2. Build game plans to deliver success.

3. Instill financial and operational disciplines.

4. Keep score based on facts.

5. Build a game-breaking organization.

6. Cultivate a "play hard and fair" culture

7. Avoid trouble

**REAL GAME, REAL PEOPLE
AN OWNER'S EXPERIENCE WITH A PABOARD**

WE FORMED AN ADVISORY BOARD TO IMPROVE OUR "GAME." WE NEEDED TO PROFESSIONALIZE OUR COMPANY AND DEAL WITH THE CONTINUING SHIFT IN OUR MARKETPLACE. WE HAD SIGNIFICANT INTERNAL ISSUES TO RESOLVE. THE ADVISORY BOARD COACHED US AS WE DEALT WITH A PARTNERSHIP ISSUE AND EVALUATED OUR TEAM.

THE ADVISORY BOARD IMMEDIATELY IDENTIFIED
THE FOLLOWING FACTORS AS CRITICAL:

1. STRATEGIC DIRECTION
2. ORGANIZATIONAL CAPABILITY AND ALIGNMENT
3. EXPECTATIONS AND ACCOUNTABILITY
4. INNOVATION MANAGEMENT
5. EXECUTION AND FOLLOW-THROUGH

THE BOARD PROCESS MOVED US TO STRONGER FINANCIAL
DISCIPLINES AND THE CREATION OF A PERFORMANCE-
BASED CULTURE. THEY PUSHED US TO REDESIGN OUR
BUSINESS DEVELOPMENT PROCESS, LEADING TO SALES
AND MARGIN GROWTH AND GREATER COMPANY VALUE.

JASON LEVIN, CEO, DOS GRINGOS

Play Like a Pro #1: Define Success

Success is defined by what outcomes the owners want and when they want to transfer the ownership of the company. The advisory board must learn the owners' definition of "What is enough? What is the value target? What terms are acceptable: all cash, cash plus stock, payment over time, or no sale but sustainable growth?" With this information, everyone knows what they must achieve to succeed.

The "when" part of the success equation drives many decisions and risk assessments. If success is selling the company is two years, the board's guidance and energy will be entirely different than if the goal is to transfer the business to family members in the distant future.

With "how much," "what" and "when" agreed to, the PABoard and management can then focus on the "how."

There are many alternatives for how to realize the valuation goals. They all have an element of risk and different implications on how to manage the business. Do the owners intend to take the company public or sell to a strategic buyer or equity investor? Do they want to transfer ownership to their employees through an employee stock ownership plan (ESOP), pursue a management buyout, or retain and build the company? The PABoard members will guide the owners and the management team through the pros and cons of each alternative and the associated risks of each.

Valuation Target Gap

Owners should project a valuation target for sustainable value during the strategic planning process. This target is a time sensitive, enterprise value forecast that will crystallize their monetary objectives. The gap between the company's historical performance trend line and the target, as depicted in the following exhibit, is then visible. The gap may be impacted by economic factors, such as inflation or strategic initiatives, which include new products, new markets, acquisitions, alliances and investments.

The gap shortfall becomes the basis for a strategic map. It is then divided into yearly and quarterly segments. These serve as a guide for the advisory board to coach management as it chooses and executes alternative strategies to reach the shareholder's value target.

Value Gap

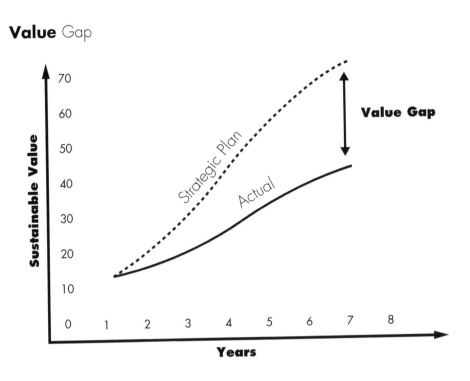

THE VISION

As it says in Proverbs 29:18, "Where there is no vision, the people perish." This Biblical axiom is still true today. The people in the company, including the board, want to know where they are going. With a clear, compelling, and achievable vision, they understand how their work fits into the future they are building. They can focus on what is important. Organizational core values, principles, beliefs, and mission guide how to reach this vision.

The vision needs to be well understood throughout the company to instill organizational coherence and market focus. It is the basis for a company's "elevator speech" that every employee can recite and support.

Play Like a Pro #2: Build a Game Plan

STRATEGIC INTENT

One of the PABoard's primary concerns is determining the strategic direction of the company. What opportunities and alternatives should the company pursue? What is a strategic game plan for the next 3 to 5 years. Hillcrest Associates, a management consulting firm, has developed a strategic planning model to help companies define a strategic direction.

Strategic Planning Model

The process begins with defining what the company wants to become—the vision of the company at least three to five years in the future. After agreement on the vision, the group defines where the company is today. That reality is reflected in the SWOT analysis (Strengths, Weaknesses, Opportunities, and Threats). With these shared definitions, the planners can define the strategic and operating objectives and action plans. Finally, the planners decide what to do next and who will do it. All of this planning is done within the framework of the company's values and mission.

PLANNING IS EVERYTHING

Dwight Eisenhower once said, "The plan is nothing. Planning is everything." The owners, management, and company's boards must have a strong sense of the winning strategic direction. The strategic planning experience defines the value drivers that are critical to meeting the owner's long-term objectives. Using the Hillcrest model, a company will identify and answer the strategic questions of "why, what, who, when and how." Companies that consistently and thoroughly plan and follow the plan with an eye on changing conditions will reap the following benefits:

❖ *Achieve or exceed revenue and profit projections.*

❖ *Advance toward a clear vision.*

❖ *Expand the company's competitive advantage.*

❖ *Leverage the company's niche.*

❖ *Build trust between owners and management.*

❖ *Improve teamwork and execution.*

❖ *Accomplish diversification breakthroughs.*

❖ Provide a strategic filter for all decisions.

❖ Create an ability to adapt to change and make game-changing moves.

In this process, management analyzes the business results by segment (i.e. products, customer, channel of distribution, geographic footprint, etc.). Depending on the breadth of the business, the team performs a SWOT analysis and builds a business strategy and plan for each business unit.

GAME-CHANGING RULES FOR STRATEGIC THINKING

Pay particular attention to this set of strategic principles as you do this planning.

1. Avoid "stuck in the middle" strategies.

2. Understand the importance of your financial strength and the staying power of your rivals.

3. Don't get in arms races, shootouts, or price wars.

4. Focus your differentiation strategy on meaningful voids in rival's quality, services, and customer relationships.

5. Drive for a long-term competitive position.

6. Define the growth engine for your business (strategic drivers).

7. Build brand equity with your customers.

8. Be relentless both offensively and defensively.

9. Become the experts by understanding the power of knowledge.

10. Don't think markets, think customers. "Never take your eye off the customer."

11. Remember, a winning strategy changes the game.

In Appendix C the authors have outlined a strategic questionnaire that can help the advisory board and owners ask the pertinent strategic questions.

BUSINESS DEVELOPMENT PLANS

Business development is the bellwether to the professional model and critical to the forecasting, budgeting, and capital allocations for a company. Board members look to the presence of a business development process that supports customer identification, acquisition, and retention. It is lead-generation oriented and encompasses a competent selling system. Companies need a discernible customer focus anchored by a meaningful value proposition and business development plans for execution.

The board also wants to see the development plan in the context of competition and industry trends. An ongoing environmental scan of political, social, and technological trends is essential.

Other aspects of a business development process include marketing plans by business segment, competitive gap analysis, and clarity on points of differentiation.

> Play Like a Pro #3: Instill Disciplines

FINANCIAL DISCIPLINE

Financial discipline is the cornerstone of a success-driven culture. The importance of profit, risk assessment, return on assets employed, consistent results, effective measurements, and reliable reporting systems become central principles of the company. These disciplines drive an organizational commitment to communication and training that manages the business around a model that meets financial expectations. It also reflects the "state of order" in your business that leads to financial success.

Financial discipline has the following objectives:

❖ Generate timely, accurate, and meaningful numbers.

❖ Sustain a profitable business.

❖ Maintain a strong cash position.

❖ Build a healthy balance sheet.

❖ Provide adequate compensation or return to owners.

❖ Deliver sustainable value that meets the owner's definition of success.

The forecasting process and resultant budget development are centerpieces to the board's oversight and effectiveness. Advisory boards can also be helpful in arranging credit lines and sourcing alternative capital. Most boards will want management to also prepare a contingency plan in order to prepare for a "midnight" event or any degree of significant demise in the revenue forecast.

To survive and build value in today's volatile environment, a company must manage its balance sheet and be cash proficient by projecting cash breakeven points on a rolling twelve-month basis. The board will monitor cash flow to ensure that the company can:

❖ Serve creditors.

❖ Reduce debt.

❖ Provide a return to the owners.

❖ *Invest in growth.*

❖ *Fund acquisitions.*

Additional financial disciplines required by the board include:

❖ Segment the profit and loss statement by customer and products/ services.

❖ Benchmark against industry standards.

❖ Install reliable direct costing systems and internal controls.

❖ Employ risk assessment processes.

❖ Deliver controlled, profitable growth.

CAPITAL STRUCTURE

A PABoard will pay close attention to the capital structure of a company. It can assist the CEO and owners in suggesting ways to negotiate the credit facilities required for a growing business. It will assist in identifying and selecting institutions that are a fit for the needs of the business.

A growing business will initially rely on a revolver/working capital line secured by accounts receivables and inventory. A term loan or senior secured debt can be used to augment longer-term needs. Most lending institutions will require a personal guarantee from the major owners. Subordinated notes or mezzanine financing can support rapid growth, acquisitions or R&D investments.

If a company is squeezed financially or runs into troubles, relief can sometimes be generated through convertible subordinated debentures or redeemable preferred stock. Most businesses will also use equipment financing or leasing to support capital investment needs.

Equity financing can be used in some circumstances, but warrants and liquidation preferences are usually required, as well as full ratchet protection and "drag along" voting rights.

As a business becomes more encumbered with debt and other fixed obligations, the cost and risk of the financial structure become magnified. Professional advisory boards will closely monitor management's use of funds to mitigate cost and risk.

MARGINS

Management and the board must focus on margins as a critical element to a company's success because it is "the game." Gross margin is a clear measure of how well you are playing the game in the marketplace. You can only obtain high gross margins if your products and services are highly valued by your customers. Low gross margins tell a board that you are just like your competitors, so you can only compete on price.

Without sustainable and improving margins, the value of a business and its very existence is in jeopardy. Boards want to see a reliable costing system and the ability to track margins by product or service segment, as well as by customer, to effectively analyze performance and opportunity.

The authors utilize a version of a model developed by Boston Consulting Group in establishing pricing strategies, culling low margin product/services, and driving enterprise value. Whether a company is considering growth alternatives through new products, new markets, new customers, or acquisitions, the guideline is that the new margins should be accretive.

Margin Contribution Analysis

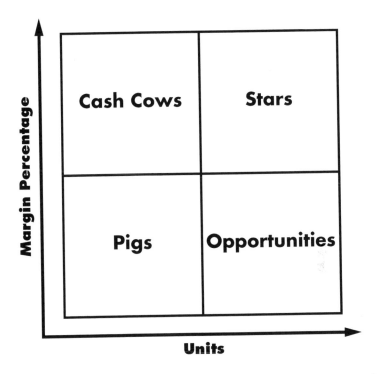

The Cash Cows are products and services that yield relatively low volume, but generate good gross margins. They also may be slow growth products that will not deliver a good return on investment if the company invested in their growth. Best strategy is to use the margins from these products for investment in Stars and Opportunities and limit investments in Pigs.

Stars are high-margin, high-volume products that have growth potential. Investing in these will yield a strong return and build the future of the business.

Opportunities can be high-unit volume products that could be redesigned to improve their margins. They probably carry a good portion of the fixed overhead allocation of the company. Losing these gross margin dollars would not be desirable. Fix them first.

Pigs are products that are low volume and low margin. Fix these immediately unless they have significant strategic value. If they cannot be fixed, they should be "culled."

EBITDA BRIDGE

The EBITDA Bridge is a powerful tool. EBITDA (earnings before interest, taxes, depreciation, and amortization) is a reporting mechanism that keeps owners and management focused on creating value. It reflects the cash flow of the business. EBITDA is forecasted yearly and then separated into quarterly increments. Management reports to the board on the deviations from the projections. Management and the board can quickly ascertain the variances from the plan, such as margin, purchases, overhead absorption, severance costs, etc.

Quarterly EBITDA Gap

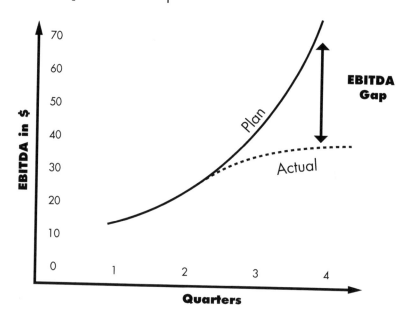

If management has a mid-year forecast for year-end earnings that are lower than planned EBITDA, it should present an action plan to "bridge the EBITDA gap" between the plan and the new forecast so that the company makes its original plan.

Play Like a Pro #4: Keep Score

OPERATIONAL DISCIPLINES AND KPIs

Even though the board will generally stay out of the "weeds" of day-to-day management, it will inquire about the efficiency of the business process and about how it is measured. The board will want to know the steps in the value chain, the effectiveness of the information technology systems and cost-reduction programs. It will ask about purchasing controls, which are the key components to margin strength and the management performance systems.

In the monthly board report, depending on the industry and company complexity, management will review operational KPIs:

EXAMPLES OF KEY PERFORMANCE INDICATORS (KPIs)

Liquidity KPIs	Sustainable Growth KPIs
Quick ratio	Return on equity
Current ratio	Return on assets
Working capital	Sustainable growth rate

Cash Management KPIs
Receivables: Days sales outstanding, Aging
Inventory: Days sales in inventory, Turns, Aging
Payables: Days outstanding, Aging

Leverage KPIs	**Coverage KPIs**
Equity in assets	EBITDA/interest
Debt/Worth	EBITDA/debt service
Debt/Tangible net worth	Bank covenant compliance

Profitability KPIs	**Growth KPIs**
Gross profit/net sales	Sales
Operating profit/sales	Assets
EBITDA percentage of sales	Liabilities
EBITDA dollars	Net Worth
Profit by business segment	Profits
	Net New Customers

Efficiency and Effectiveness KPIs
Revenue/Employee
Net income/employee
Inventory turnover
Receivable days sales outstanding
Return on equity
Operations on-time and complete shipments
New customer acquisition
Dollars per sales transaction
Customer satisfaction ratings

METRICS DASHBOARD USES

COLLECTING DATA IS MECHANICAL AND MEANINGLESS.
WHAT COUNTS IS WHAT YOU DO WITH IT.

WE CONDENSE DATA INTO A HANDFUL OF KEY INDICATORS,
WHICH MEASURE THINGS THAT ARE CRITICAL TO OUR SUCCESS.
WE THEN SHARE THIS INFORMATION WIDELY. IF ASSOCIATES
KNOW HOW THEY AND THEIR BUSINESS UNITS ARE DOING,
THEY CAN CHANGE THEIR BEHAVIOR AND THEIR RESULTS.

PEOPLE LEARN IN DIFFERENT WAYS, SO WE USE E-MAIL,
POSTINGS, NEWSLETTERS, AND IN-PERSON PRESENTATIONS.
SALES AND GROSS PROFIT NUMBERS ARE E-MAILED TO
ALL EMPLOYEES EVERY DAY. PERFORMANCE METRICS
SUCH AS ON-TIME DELIVERY, BACK-ORDERS, AND
RETURNS, ETC. ARE PUBLISHED MONTHLY. ALSO, AT
MONTH END, WE POST MEASUREMENTS OF SAFETY,
FINANCIAL PERFORMANCE, CUSTOMER SURVEYS, SYSTEM
IMPROVEMENTS, AND EMPLOYEE DEVELOPMENT ACTIVITY.

EACH QUARTER, WE SHARE THE SAME KEY INDICATORS
WITH THE BOARD. TWICE A YEAR WE VISIT WITH ALL
EMPLOYEES AND DISCUSS THE CHARTS AND DATA
PICTURES THAT MEASURE OUR PERFORMANCE.

MANAGEMENT AND BRANCH BONUSES ARE TIED TO
PERFORMANCE MEASURED BY SEVERAL OF THE KEY INDICATORS
THAT CAN BE CONTROLLED BY THAT PERSON OR UNIT.

ERIC STEINHAUER
PRESIDENT, INDUSTRIAL METAL SUPPLY

The board will insist that the following business processes are in place to ensure operational discipline:

- ❖ *Annual operational plans*
- ❖ *Departmental standards*
- ❖ *Lean manufacturing process*
- ❖ *Effective purchasing processes*
- ❖ *Contribution margin analysis*
- ❖ *Clear systems and procedures*

> **Play Like a Pro #5: Build a Game-Breaker Organization**

ORGANIZATIONAL STRUCTURE AND DESIGN

The board provides oversight on the company's organizational structure and design. It is very interested in attracting talent, company culture, succession planning, and effective training programs. The board wants a structure and process that provides all employees with the opportunity to excel. It wants a team in place that can execute the tactical and strategic plans.

The board will always coach an organization on how to have a strong bench of qualified people who can grow the business. The board wants to see game-breaker executives in the key functional roles. The strongest teams are developed by growing their current people; however, performance is often accelerated by adding professional management to these game-breaker positions.

CEO Role

The importance of the CEO's role cannot be overstated. He or she is the key to playing the game well. The CEO has five areas of leadership that must be managed to create success:

- ❖ **Meaning.** The CEO defines for the team the higher meaning of the business. This could be called the mission statement. Everyone needs to know and embrace why the company is in business from a customer's point of view.

- ❖ **Attention.** Of all the decisions that need to be made and the actions to take, which ones are most important? Which ones create the most value or preserve the value of the company?

- ❖ **Trust.** Companies whose employees trust each other are more profitable and move faster than those whose trust is low. The CEO must establish policies and lead a culture that builds trust, and then demonstrate that he is trustworthy.

- ❖ **Culture.** The CEO works with the team to define "how we do things and treat people around here." Employees see these principles as the culture or style of the company. They watch to see if management's actions fit the culture they talk about.

- ❖ **Actions.** Great leaders make things happen. They lead the team to make good and timely decisions and take action.

BOARD MENTORING OF THE CEO

OF THE MANY ROLES BOARDS PLAY, THE BALANCING OF OVERSIGHT WITH SUPPORT OF MANAGEMENT CAN CREATE SOME OF THE GREATEST CHALLENGES. ONE OFTEN OVERLOOKED SUPPORT OPPORTUNITY BOARDS HAVE TO ADD VALUE TO SHAREHOLDERS IS THE FORMAL OR INFORMAL MENTORING OF THE CEO. BOARD MEMBERS ARE SELECTED BASED ON THEIR CREDIBILITY, WISDOM, AND EXPERIENCE. APPLYING THESE QUALITIES IN ONE-ON-ONE COUNSEL AND MENTORING WITH THE CEO CAN LEAD TO MEASURABLY MORE THOUGHTFUL AND EFFECTIVE LEADERSHIP AND DECISIONS.

> MENTORING IS A RELATIONSHIP, SO THE DIRECTOR(S)
> DOING THE MENTORING MUST HAVE THE TIME AND INTEREST
> AS WELL AS THE TRUST AND CONFIDENCE OF THE CEO,
> AND VICE-VERSA. TO BE EFFECTIVE IN CREATING CHANGE,
> THE CEO MUST SEEK AND BE OPEN TO THE MENTORING.
> TRANSPARENCY AMONG THE BOARD MEMBERS ABOUT THE
> MENTORING RELATIONSHIP IS ESSENTIAL, AS IS AGREEMENT
> ON CONFIDENTIALITY ABOUT THE TOPICS DISCUSSED.
>
> DICK FONTAINE, COACH AND FORMER DAVITA
> BOARD OF DIRECTORS MEMBER

WHO IS ON THE TEAM?

Advisory boards should always focus on the capabilities of the CEO and senior management team. You cannot win the game without "game breakers" in every key functional position. The board may ask these questions about the team and its teamwork:

- ❖ Are the major shareholder, CEO, and senior management team driven and passionate about success? Are they willing to make the tough decisions to get to their goals?

- ❖ Are the major shareholder, CEO, and senior management team accountable, visible, and do they promote an intense performance environment?

- ❖ Is compensation tied to intense organizational performance?

- ❖ Is the hiring environment one of attitude, integrity, and sound judgment?

- ❖ Does the leadership set the example at all levels?

❖ Is there a sense of organizational trust, and are company values openly communicated?

❖ Is the CEO a hands-on leader without elites or sacred cows?

❖ Are there real opportunities for growth and advancement?

Play Like a Pro #6: Strong Culture

The "Play Hard and Fair" Culture

There is a powerful, anonymous quotation: "Culture eats strategy for lunch every day." The early part of this chapter talks about how to define, measure, and play the game. Your company's culture determines if any of these plans and action items will produce results.

A "play hard and fair" culture answers everyone's question: "How do we play the game around here?" The culture informs the team on what actions to take or not take. It defines how to act toward fellow players, customers, competitors, and vendors. It creates the criteria for the people selected to join the team. The culture encompasses such elements as:

1. Demanding standards of professional conduct

2. Commitment to tangible results and profits

3. Open communications

4. Honesty

5. Strong code of ethics

6. Working hard and smart

7. High levels of trust

8. Continuous learning

9. Fair compensation based on results

10. Customer focus

11. Collaboration and teamwork

12. Personal growth and financial reward

The mere presence of an advisory board in the governance of a private company will strengthen a culture of expected performance and professionalism. The board will ask:

❖ Why are you in business? Tell us your mission or purpose from the customer's point of view. Do your employees understand and embrace this mission?

❖ What are the values that we follow as we pursue this mission? How do we treat each other and the customer?

❖ What does success look like for the customer, the company, and the people who build it?

Everyone will know that the PABoard pays attention to the way things get done. This attention and the related accountabilities will provide the owners and CEO with positive reinforcement to build and promote a great culture.

Management implements culture through leadership teams and one-on-one coaching. There is a continuous learning conversations and employee recognition based on behavior that is consistent with the elements of the culture.

A winning culture is reinforced through performance-based compensation and implemented using realistic measurements, performance dashboards, and a fair review process.

NINE WAYS TO EVALUATE YOUR COMPANY CULTURE

1. Is your company a sought-after employer?

2. Is there a positive team environment?

3. Are there clear expectations?

4. Is there an organizational sense of urgency?

5. Is it a learning organization?

6. Is there a multi-level coaching environment?

7. Is there an effective communication process?

8. Does the organization embrace change?

9. Is there inherent positive energy?

DECISION MAKING AND ACTION

If all the elements of this chapter are present, you will have an effective organization that plays the game well. It consistently makes the right decisions at the right time and takes the right actions. The processes of defining the intended outcomes, planning, setting goals, measuring and communicating performance, and delivering timely feedback give people the information they need to make good decisions.

The "play hard and fair" culture is led by a management team that models professional values and behaviors. It shows the team how to make decisions and operate the business.

The oversight of the board and its processes help ensure strategic and high-level operating decisions. The PABoard process requires that leadership step back from the day-to-day activity every quarter to examine why they are in business, where they are going, and how they are getting there. The CEO and the senior management manage the culture to deliver results and work with their people. They must judge their decisions and actions against the board's mission of building sustainable value in the company.

The net result of playing the game well is better decisions and greater value.

Play Like a Pro #7: Avoid Trouble

AVOID TROUBLE

Here are eight behavioral areas that can hamper a business. If the leadership loses their sensitivity to these, the company may not play the game well:

1. *Ignoring balance sheet trends: Working capital erosion*

2. *Squeeze play: Borrowing long-term for short-term needs*

3. *Forgetting the business model: What are the core strengths? What got us here?*

4. *Failing to look down the track: Asking "what if?"*

5. *Hanging on to old stuff: Avoidance of change*

6. *Losing touch with the customer: CEO not interacting with customers*

7. *Forgetting the anthill: Failure to solicit input from the internal team*

8. *Eroding trust and commitment: Regularly missing forecasts and lack of accountability*

The Advisory Board Wants to Know:

The fundamentals described in this chapter are necessary for success. As part of their process, PABoards will drill down to ensure these fundamentals are in place as part of the value-building journey. Sustainable value will not be created unless this infrastructure and organizational competency is in place. Here are some questions the PABoard will ask about how you play the game:

1. Is the vision for the future of the company clearly defined and agreed to by the owners, management, and the board?

2. Does the company have strategic, operating, and budget plans?

3. Does management manage to these plans and consistently deliver the promised results?

4. Are key performance indicators defined and measured accurately on a timely basis?

5. Does the company have a "game breaker" person in each key position?

6. Does the decision-making process deliver consistently good and timely decisions?

7. Is the technology leading, lagging, or current with customers and internal needs? What investment is needed?

8. Is the culture a "play hard and fair" culture as defined in the corporate mission and values, and is it reinforced by the reward system and being modeled by the CEO and the management team?

9. Is this a company where people can grow financially and professionally and enjoy their working environment?

CHAPTER 7

The Sustainable Value Game

"A business that makes nothing but money is a poor business."
Henry Ford

Every owner wants to know, "What is my company worth?" There are so many types of buyers, valuation approaches, and deal terms that the real world answer is, "Whatever you and a willing buyer agree on."

The authors have served on many boards of companies that were sold. Collectively, they delivered over $1.1 billion to the owners. The valuations ranged from a company with no profit that sold for four times revenue to companies that sold for two times earnings and others that were valued from seven to twelve times earnings. Why do companies sell for such a wide range of value?

To understand valuations you must understand the buyers and what they value, the market and its attractiveness, a company's sustainable value, and the definition of EBITDA.

BUYERS AND APPROACHES

Buyers come from all over the world and from many disciplines. Some of them are:

- ❖ Competitors or strategic buyers
- ❖ Private equity funds
- ❖ Your management team
- ❖ Private investors
- ❖ Public companies
- ❖ International groups
- ❖ General public through public stock offerings

These different buyers/investors usually have their own transactional approaches using a combination of the following methodologies to define valuation:

- ❖ Industry comparables and sector conditions
- ❖ Quality and sustainability of earnings
- ❖ Standard practice value determinants
- ❖ Strategic growth expectations and fit
- ❖ Value enhancements

INDUSTRY COMPARATIVES AND INDUSTRY CONDITIONS

Every industry, in an investment banker's vernacular, has a range of earnings or revenue multiples that are reasonably predicated by prior transactions. These multiples establish a valuation guidance range for the buyer or investor.

Buyers and equity investors, in conjunction with prior transaction guidance, will review the current industry and sector conditions to evaluate:

❖ Economic cycles

❖ Barriers to entry

❖ Governmental policy impact

❖ Competitive actions

❖ Technological threats

❖ Potential logistical and distribution challenges

In addition, they will exhaust all other due-diligence factors to assess their investment alternatives and risks.

QUALITY OF EARNINGS

Every valuation of a company is based on trust in the future profitability of the business model. Investment bankers and private equity groups often label this trust as "quality of earnings." If the past earnings of a company have been erratic or have depended on singular events, a few customers, or government windfalls, then the quality or predictability of future earnings is low. If the past earnings were based on sales that deliver high and constant gross margin from a variety of customers who all signed long-term contracts, the quality of earnings would tend to be high. If an investor can have full transparency of financial transactions, visibility of profitability by customer and product line, and can see how to manage key variables, the belief in the quality of earnings and predictability increases again.

Many components roll up into an outsider's assessment of earnings quality. A PABoard process helps the shareholders define those components. The board will push management to operate the business so that its quality of earnings continues to improve.

If the company has a high quality of earnings, it probably will receive at least another "turn" on its evaluation. Another "turn" means that the valuation multiplier can move from 4.0 to 5.0 times EBITDA. For a company with $5 million in EBITDA, this means their sustainable value will increase from $20 million to $25 million.

EBITDA Is Not EBITDA

In this book and throughout every business book, you see EBITDA used as if it is an easily measured figure. It would be easy to assume that EBITDA is earnings, plus interest paid, plus taxes paid, plus depreciation, plus any amortization taken by the company. Logically, all these measures would be made to conform to commonly accepted accounting principles. It would then be easy for any sophisticated buyer and seller to agree on the EBITDA and multiply it by an evaluation multiplier that is the industry norm to get the value of the company...more or less.

And there is the rub—the more or less.

In every sale of a company, there comes the time when the buyer says something like, "I think we need to adjust the EBITDA to reflect a proper depreciation schedule." Or, "Your interest payments are made on working capital, and that varies dramatically by quarter, so I think we need to adjust the EBITDA to reflect the normalized interest payment schedule." Or the seller says, "I took a higher salary than the industry norm, so this EBITDA should be adjusted to reflect what would be paid to a normal executive after you buy it." Or an accountant says, "That is the EBITDA today, but in two years we will be on the international accounting system. Then the EBITDA will need to be adjusted."

Notice the word "adjusted" in each of those sentences?

A major part of the value of any sale is determined by the negotiation between buyer and seller on what is the true EBITDA. After the accountants and valuation firms on both sides have excluded and added back earnings, they arrive at their EBITDA number.

EBITDA is not EBITDA until both buyer and seller agree on the number.

STANDARD PRACTICE METHODOLOGY

Most experienced buyers and investors will employ an external valuation firm to justify purchase prices to boards, investment funds, and senior lenders. They will use a methodology or standard practice that they have established over a series of transactions that has proven to support their pre-established acquisition or investment filter. Common financial techniques they might consider:

❖ *EBITDA multiples*

❖ *Book value multiples*

❖ *Revenue multiples*

❖ *Net asset value*

❖ *Liquidation value*

❖ *Discounted cash flow*

❖ *Internal rate of return*

STRATEGIC GROWTH POTENTIAL

The growth potential of the business being considered is critical to both strategic buyers and investors. Projected growth in earnings will determine the company's probability of meeting return on investment (ROI) criteria or debt service needs. Buyers want to understand the best predictions on future growth rates in each product offering and market segment. They will want to know the company's performance history and if it can be accelerated by the infusion of additional resources. They will judge the probability of management's ability to achieve their strategic plan.

ACHIEVING STRONG SUSTAINABLE VALUE

The first priority of the PABoard is to guide the company and its management so that the company is valued much more highly than "standard practices" or industry "standards" would dictate.

Buyers buy much more than past financial performance or assets. They buy what they believe to be the future of the company. They will pay you an amount equal to several or even many years of past earnings if they believe in you and your company.

The authors have developed a model called "The Sustainable Value Wheel." It is the framework that PABoards should use to coach a business to growing its value. .

The Sustainable Value Wheel represents the entity that a buyer buys. At its core are financial measures. The sectors around the core are non-financial factors that build trust in the future and affect the value. They either add to or detract from the multiple that will be paid. The goal of the board is to drive a process that leads to high ratings in each sector. A strong core of good financials and highly performing outer ring factors creates strong Sustainable Value.

Sustainable Value Wheel

VALUE FACTORS

After observing numerous transactions in which companies were sold, the authors have identified 15 significant value factors that are most often used to determine transferable value. These factors will impact the value of a business when it is evaluated by buyers or investors. Some of these are non-financial factors, but they speak to the quality of earnings. When these value factors are fully developed, buyers have paid extraordinary multiples for every dollar of EBITDA earned.

Here are the 15 value factors shown in the Sustainable Value Wheel:

1. EBITDA dollars and percentage of sales
2. Gross margin strength
3. CEO leadership
4. Business disciplines
5. Management information
6. Attractive industry
7. Growth model
8. "Must have" company
9. Productive culture
10. Management team
11. Customer Relationships
12. Diverse customers
13. Diversified products and markets
14. Size of revenue and profits
15. Technology and intellectual property

Each buyer or investor may put a different weight on these value factors. If a buyer wants your technology, he may not care about the management team. Or if the buyer is a private equity entity, he may give extra weight to the management team because the buyer is not an operator.

EBITDA

As discussed earlier, "EBITDA isn't EBITDA until buyer and seller agree on the number." It is one of the strongest considerations in valuing a company, although companies have been sold for millions of dollars with no EBITDA at all. Think of all the dot-com companies that went public even when they had tremendous losses, and they still delivered billions in shareholder value.

However, it is obvious that companies that produce consistent EBITDA percentages over several years and whose EBITDA can be realistically projected to continue, deliver significant value to their owners.

GROSS MARGINS

Gross margin percentages are the measure of a company's uniqueness in the market place. High gross margin is proof that a customer is willing to pay well above a company's costs because they want the product, and there is a lack of competitors who can deliver the same product or service.

If your gross margin percentage (gross margin dollars divided by sales dollars times 100 percent) can withstand the assault of competitive bidding or customer buying pressure to reduce price, this will be demonstrated in stable or increasing gross margins over time. Gross margins speak to your ability to create better ways to serve customer needs while controlling internal costs or by innovating your processes and products.

Buyers and investors will move away from companies whose gross margin dollars or gross margin percentages are declining or are weaker than industry averages. They will be very interested in gross margin dollars and percentages that are increasing even in tough times.

STRONG CEO LEADERSHIP

The authors were tempted to bold this entire section for emphasis. Unless your company's value is centered on a defensible patent, an unbreakable contract, or some other unusually valuable asset, the game breaker for valuation is the CEO and, to a lesser extent, the senior management team. All the ratios, relationships, and past performance have little impact on the future if the leadership of the company is not competent, passionate, engaged, aligned, and presentable to those who are valuing the business. The right CEO and team inspire confidence, attract money, create opportunities, and develop resources for the business. They are the game changers.

A mediocre business with a great CEO and management team will be worth more in the marketplace and attract more capital than an excellent business with a weak CEO and management team. Great products without strong business leadership are worth the value of the intellectual property, but not worth much as a future business.

The critical question for the business owner, who may have started the business or grown up in it, is, "Am I the CEO others would trust to double or triple the size and earnings of this business, or should that be someone else?" Several related questions reflect on the valuation: "Do I have the skills, energy, and desire to grow the business? Do I have the management style that would allow me to work for a new owner if I sold?" Do I have the right management team to reach the strategic goals?

An investor wants a CEO whom they can trust to stay after a sale, who has a proven record of growing companies, and who knows how to plan and manage a business in a style that satisfies a board or outside investor's demands. Most founders of middle- market companies are not that person. They may possess some of the characteristics of that leader, but often they cannot fully convince themselves or others that they are that leader or that they will stay after a sale.

REAL GAME, REAL PEOPLE

TOM MURPHY, MANAGING PARTNER OF M&A CAPITAL, COMMENTED ON THE SUSTAINABLE VALUE WHEEL: "IN THIS MODEL, THERE ARE TWO SECTORS THAT ARE BY FAR THE MOST IMPORTANT IN OUR DECISION TO FINANCE A COMPANY: THE CEO LEADERSHIP AND THE ATTRACTIVE INDUSTRY. WHEN WE FIND A GREAT CEO IN THE RIGHT INDUSTRY, THAT IS WHERE WE WILL INVEST. A GREAT CEO WILL MAKE ALL THE OTHER SECTORS WORK."

If you decide to bring in an outside CEO, the authors recommend that the owner/founder find and train an outside CEO for at least two years before a sale. If the CEO has two years of proven track record, buyers will give full value to that value factor and to the company. The reasons for this recommendation are:

❖ Investors want to invest in a CEO who will probably stay for three years or more. The average private-company owner or founder, who sells, stays with the new owners less than 12 months.

❖ An outside CEO who has "been there and done that" in a larger company can inspire investments from banks, investors, and other financial institutions better than a CEO who has "not done that."

❖ If the new CEO has been in place for two years, he has had time to prove that he can run and grow the business and create a team to run it within his leadership style. This inspires trust from outsiders because it makes the new person a proven entity.

❖ Outside CEOs, particularly ones from larger companies, develop professional reporting systems, financial measurements, and key indicator tracking that adds to investors comfort and trust.

Here is a story of a company that dominated its niche of aerospace replacement parts, built an excellent management team, and created an extraordinary return for its owners.

REAL GAME, REAL PEOPLE

MY SISTER AND I PURCHASED A TROUBLED SURPLUS AIRCRAFT PARTS COMPANY FROM OUR FATHER TWENTY-FIVE YEARS AGO. OVER THE YEARS WE TRANSFORMED THE BUSINESS FROM SURPLUS DISTRIBUTION TO MANUFACTURING. WE MANUFACTURED EQUIPMENT UNDER LICENSE AGREEMENTS WITH THE ORIGINAL OEMs.

WE USED AN ADVISORY BOARD TO HELP US TRIPLE THE VALUE OF OUR BUSINESS IN THE LAST THREE YEARS AND SELL IT. HERE IS WHAT WE DID

THE FIRST STEP WE TOOK WAS TO HIRE A CEO. WE CREATED A THOROUGH PROCESS FOR THIS TASK AND EXECUTED IT INTERNALLY. WE WERE VERY SUCCESSFUL.

OUR SECOND STEP WAS TO ESTABLISH A BOARD OF ADVISORS. WE WANTED THE BOARD TO ADVISE US ON THE SALE PREPARATION AND SALE PROCESS AS WELL AS TO HELP US GOVERN OUR NEW CEO. NEITHER OF US HAD HAD A CEO REPORTING TO US PREVIOUSLY. WE WERE NERVOUS ABOUT HANDING OVER THE REINS TO OUR COMPANY.

IN HINDSIGHT, WE SHOULD HAVE SET UP THE BOARD FIRST. THEY COULD HAVE BEEN VERY VALUABLE IN HIRING THE CEO.

THE BOARD HELPED US IDENTIFY AND FOCUS ON THE VALUE DRIVERS OF OUR BUSINESS. OUR BOARD SET UP A VALUE CREATION PLAN. WE STARTED BY IDENTIFYING POTENTIAL BUYER TYPES. THEN WE LISTED ATTRIBUTES THESE BUYERS WOULD VALUE. MOST OF THESE ATTRIBUTES ARE OBVIOUS, BUT SOME NOT SO OBVIOUS.

FOR EACH OF THE VALUES THAT WE FELT WE COULD SIGNIFICANTLY IMPACT, WE CREATED A PLAN. WE THEN ENSURED THAT THESE PLANS WERE INCORPORATED WITH OUR STRATEGIC, MARKETING, AND SALES PLANS. WE HAD KEY INDICATORS RELATED TO EACH VALUE.

THIS WAS A VERY POWERFUL EXERCISE. IT EFFECTIVELY REFOCUSED OUR ENTIRE ORGANIZATION AROUND CREATING VALUE IN ANTICIPATION OF THE SALE OF THE COMPANY. AT THE SAME TIME, ONLY OUR BOARD AND TRANSACTION TEAMS KNEW WHAT THE END GAME WAS.

THIS CAUSED US TO MAKE MANY CHANGES, INCLUDING:

1. CHANGING OUT MOST OF OUR MIDDLE MANAGEMENT
2. HIRING A CEO TO REPLACE OURSELVES
3. INVESTING HEAVILY IN NEW PRODUCT LINES
4. REPLACING OUR ERP SYSTEM
5. REVISING OUR INCENTIVE PROGRAMS TO FOCUS ON OUR VALUE DRIVERS
6. ALIGNING MY SISTER AND ME TO GET ON THE SAME PAGE AS THE BOARD AND STAY THERE
7. HIRING AN EXCELLENT M&A ADVISOR

THESE ACTIONS ALL TRANSLATED INTO TRIPLING THE VALUE OF OUR COMPANY.

TED ALLRED, PRESIDENT OF ONTIC AND
TERESA ALLRED, CEO OF ONTIC

BUSINESS DISCIPLINES

Business disciplines and processes speak to the company's ability to manage costs, deliver consistent quality, and drive innovation in their internal processes. One of the foundational pieces of Walmart's dominance is its operational efficiency. Its distribution costs are about two percentage points lower than its competitors' costs. Apple is seen to have a strong discipline of innovation. Amazon and Google have the powerful discipline of customer data and knowledge. What is the internal discipline that will add value to your company?

The planning process is a key discipline. The company should be committed to an annual cycle of developing a strategic plan, which includes plans for each business function. The annual business and operating plan is tied to the strategic objectives in the strategic plan. Department plans are aligned with these overall plans. Personal action and incentives are tied to both plans, as are incentive plans.

These planning disciplines are backed up with processes that ensure that the plans are executed consistently and efficiently. Metrics monitor the processes. Communication disciplines ensure timely, accurate gathering and dissemination of information.

Operational disciplines in production are the key to profitability, both profit gross margins and net earnings. Buying practices, lean production processes, high levels of training, and proper use of technology all contribute to delivering high levels of sustainable profits.

Financial disciplines are essential. Issue monthly financial reports within ten days of the end of the month. Cash forecasts should look out thirteen weeks. Controls on checks need to be in place. Have a set of financial KPIs and manage to them. The board and the accountants will give you guidelines and tracking metrics.

All these disciplines and more are guided by the overarching discipline of the company creating and living by a rigorous set of values and ethics.

MANAGEMENT INFORMATION SYSTEMS

Many companies seem to make major investments in their information and technology systems about every five to seven years. Between these big changes, they modify and update. If your company is offered for sale, the state of your information systems may become an issue. Will the buyer have to spend $2 million and two disruptive years to bring your system up to industry standards, or are you a leader in this area? Can your management team and line operators get the information they need to make accurate and timely decisions now? Can you see the profitability of all your products and services and customers with your current system? How about "cloud" connections with the entities in your supply chain and customer base?

Your systems should be a strong plank in your growth platform. They should support the efficient scalability of your business.

Growth Model

Investors buy companies so they can grow them and get a large return on their investment. They often value them as platform companies that support acquisitions or as leaders in growth markets, or for their ability to create innovative products. They will pay an owner seven to ten times the current year's earning, or more, to have the opportunity to grow the company and its value. If you can prove that your infrastructure, people, supply chain, technology, and products are sound building blocks for controllable growth, then the investor will value your company more highly. He will see where he can invest to grow the business not fix the business.

Scalability is a term often applied to the growth model for software companies. The authors were aware of a software company that made a 20 percent EBITDA, was growing at 20 percent a year and had no debt. The software core of the business was highly efficient and effective when applied to current customer needs. The owners were satisfied with their current income, but they wanted to sell for three times the revenue. This could not happen soon because the software for their SAS model was not scalable. It was two generations old. In order for the company to be scalable and for buyers to see it as current, the owners had to reinvest in their technology so that it would link to all potential customers' technology. In order to sell the company for three times revenue, the owners had to invest $1.5 million in technology redesign and prove its effectiveness. The new technology was scalable, and the sustainable value of the company more than doubled.

ATTRACTIVE INDUSTRY

A dollar of EBITDA in the aerospace market might be worth about ten dollars to a buyer. In the software business, a dollar of EBITDA could be worth twenty dollars to a buyer (or three times sales). But, a dollar of earnings in the distribution business might only be worth four dollars in selling price.

Look at the multiples of earnings per share that are paid for shares on the New York Stock Exchange. They are all different depending on which market sector is in favor that particular quarter. Which sectors is the government supporting or attacking? Which markets have justifiable, long-term growth potential? The stronger the perception of the future of a market, the more capital it will attract.

As you invest your company's time and money, first ask yourself, "Are we in the right industry and industry segment to get a good return on our efforts?" Talk with an investment banker and get his or her input from an investor's point of view. Get the same input from your banker to see if the industry and that segment are bankable. Include this thinking in your strategic planning.

If the outside world will pay a reasonable multiple for companies in the industry you are in, look deeper to see which segments of your industry are valued most highly. If you are in retailing, for example, are investors paying more for high-end retailers, low-end retailers, or specialty retailers? Do they value online versus brick and mortar retailers? Continue to focus on the attractive industries and segments you can dominate.

"Must Have" Company

Many private equity groups and buyers have this measurement as one of their top investment criteria. Middle-market companies can achieve this status in niche markets through product, service, technological strength, or geographic strength. If an investor or competitor wants to enter that market, it can build a capability, which can take years and a large investment and, in the end, might fail. The most reasonable business strategy for the investor or competitor is to buy a strong, "must have" company.

One of the authors owned a franchise company that built the Penguin's Frozen Yogurt chain. It had over seventy stores in Southern California. An East Coast competitor wanted to enter the West Coast market quickly. It would have taken them three years to find good retail sites and at least that long to build up the brand awareness enjoyed by the Penguin's chain. Penguin's was then a "must have" company to fulfill the competitor's strategic objectives of West Coast distribution. The purchase also would damage the buyer's biggest competitor who was an important supplier to Penguins. They purchased Penguin's for a price that was a multiple of revenue, not EBITDA. It was called a "strategic buy" because it was a "must have" company that fit the geographic and competitive strategy of the buyer.

The authors have seen companies achieve this unique and valuable status through patented products, unique real estate holdings, long-term contracts with industry-leading clients, vendor alliances, and unequalled brand loyalty in niche markets.

Culture

The leader of an acquisitive company who had acquired over fifteen companies told the authors:

> After all the financial analysis, the most important factor in our decision to buy or walk away is the company culture. If it fits our culture, then we proceed with our due diligence. Our culture of growth, speed, intensive customer focus, and service is our formula for success. If we bring a company into our family and the people in that company have a different culture or one that has lower measures on these fundamentals, the merger will fail or be very distracting. Cultural fit is a go or no-go factor for us.

The culture of a company is difficult to define. What does "culture" mean and what does "strong" mean? Culture is a way of describing the style in which things get done in a company. It can be shaped by written values, but more importantly, by the beliefs and behaviors of the leaders. It defines what is important. It shapes how the team will act with each other and the customer. It defines who will be hired, how people will be rewarded, and who will be promoted.

> **"CULTURE EATS STRATEGY FOR LUNCH EVERY DAY."**
> **ANONYMOUS**

If your sustainable value plan shows high growth and your team is conservative and complacent, the growth will not happen. If you want to build a culture that is metrics and accountability driven and the owner says, "We are a caring, family business and we always take care of our own," then metrics and accountability will not be an important part of your culture.

"Strong culture" means different things to different investors or buyers. To a strategic buyer, a culture is strong if it fits his or her culture. Over 70 percent of mergers fail to meet the expectations of the buyer, according to published sources. The major reason for the underperformance is the lack of fit and integration of cultures of the merging entities. Usually, the larger entity's culture wins. The acquired company's team is expected to behave like the buying company. If it does not, employees are let go, or they leave because they know they do not fit in. The asset the buyer wanted now walks out the door. Value declines.

Great cultural fit to a financial buyer may have a different meaning. The buyer is not fitting his company into another operating company. But, the culture still needs to be attractive to the buyer. He has to believe the culture will drive profitability, or he will not invest. He has to believe the culture will survive if the owner or leader leaves. He wants a culture that will focus on profitable service to the company's customers, has a high sense of urgency, is under control, and will keep the critical people in the company happy.

If a company has a highly functioning PABoard, an investor knows the culture supports openness, challenge, professional reporting, planning, and accountability. This governance structure tells people inside and outside the company that this culture is based on behaviors that are logical, consistent, and value driven.

MANAGEMENT TEAM

The management team without the owner is very important to any investor. If the owner receives a significant payout when the company is sold, then the management team becomes even more important because most buyers will assume that the owners will leave within one year after a buyout. There should be a proven successor for the owner in the management team. This gives everyone more certainty that the company will continue to function well even if the owner leaves. That raises the belief in sustainability and success of the business.

One of the PABoard's highest priorities is to ensure that a succession plan is in place for each of the key executives. The plan usually includes a management development section and a formal management evaluation program.

Finally, the management team should "show well." If your company is being sold, the buyer will meet with the management team, including the owner/CEO early in the process. Often the buyer will send a functional acquisition team as part of the due diligence process. These buyer team members will meet with their counterparts in your company so they can evaluate them. If your team "shows well," the buyer has greater confidence in the future of the business, which translates to higher valuations.

The ultimate test for the value added by the management team comes during the management presentations to investors or buyers.

According to Ted Allred, when he and his sister sat in these presentations, "The buyers did not ask us any strategic operational questions. They asked the management team. The buyers' confidence rose or fell and our value rose or fell based on their confidence in the team because they believed that we would leave after the purchase was completed. They were right."

CUSTOMER RELATIONSHIPS

If a company is serving the needs of its customers better than the competition and is a good value in the customers' eyes, the customers do not leave; therefore, a key indicator of predictable revenues and margins is the company's ability to retain and grow current customers. If there is a high "churn" of customers, an investor will downgrade his valuation of the business. If customers are retained only by reducing margins, the value of the company is affected.

When a potential investor interviews your customers as the last stage of due diligence, what will your customers say about their long-term commitment to you, your team, and your company?

DIVERSE PRODUCTS AND CUSTOMERS

This factor feeds the perception of quality of earnings because it predicts the stability and resiliency of the business. Most companies start with one or two products and one customer. This is not a stable, predictable business. At this stage, loss of one customer or one product probably means the company is out of business.

Lack of diversification in customers and products lowers valuations. Suppose that a company had $10 million in sales and made

$1 million in profit last year. Would you pay $5 million for the company if you were an investor? What if we told you that it only had one customer who was struggling? Also, what if the company has not added a significant new customer for the past three years? Would you still pay $5 million for the company or would you reduce your price or change the terms of your purchase? Probably, you would pay less and pay over time because of lack of diversification and, therefore, low trust in the future.

A good guideline for adequate diversification is that no customer or product class should account for more that 10 percent of your volume or profits. If you meet that guideline, your valuations could be two turns higher than a company with lower diversification.

SIZE OF REVENUE AND EBITDA THRESHOLD

A rule of thumb is that a company's value multiplier goes up at least another turn when EBITDA passes $10 million. Why $10 million? Because $10 million is a breaking point in valuation for the investment community. A $10 million EBITDA company is much more "bankable" than an $8 million company. Below $10 million is too small for many investor groups because the fees from a transaction are small and it may be difficult to sell. Small EBITDA means the company is vulnerable to the whims of the market, to banking challenges, and to swings in valuation.

Roll-up companies and private equity groups follow these guidelines. This is one way they build value for their companies and allow the owners to retain some ownership after a buyout. Here is an example:

Two medical device companies each have $6 million in EBITDA. Individually, they may have a six times EBITDA valuation multiplier ($36 million) because they are small in investment market terms. The total valuation for the two separate companies would be $36 million plus $36 million or $72 million. If they merge or are bought and put together by an investor, their combined EBITDA is $12 million. Because their EBITDA is over $10 million, their multiplier has increased. It may be as high as eight times. So, instead of a $72 million value (six times the individual EBITDAs), the combined value is $96 million ($12 million EBITDA times eight). That could be a $24 million valuation gain just from combining two companies.

Factor	Company A	Company B	Total Stand-Alone Value	Merged Companies Valuation
EBITDA	$6M	$6M	$12M	$12M
Multiplier	6X	6X	**6X**	**8X**
Total Value	$36M	$36M	**$72M**	**$96M**

The board and investors will guide this value creation thinking in private companies whose owners are considering growth through acquisition or merger. If acquisitions make business sense, then the disproportionate pay off in higher valuation comes when the company either acquires or grows its EBITDA past $10 million.

TECHNOLOGY AND INTELLECTUAL PROPERTY

Your company must be current with the technology of the industry and the customers it serves. This requires constant evolution and maintenance of the core technologies of the company. If you are not current, the buyer will have to invest in the changes to support the company's future.

With the current move toward "cloud computing" and technologies resident on the Internet, it will be harder to have a sustainable asset in your technology. The value often will be in your use of that technology in unique and powerful ways.

If your technology is proprietary, protect it with trademarks, copyrights, or other forms of legal structure. Consult your intellectual property attorney to ensure that you have protection.

Register other intellectual property, such as brand names, in as many countries as you can afford. With the globalization of markets and buyers, your registrations in non-USA countries may hold considerable value. Again, talk to an IP attorney.

REAL GAME, REAL PEOPLE

BOARDS HAVE A PRIMARY RESPONSIBILITY TO PROTECT AND GROW THE VALUE OF A COMPANY. OFTEN INTELLECTUAL PROPERTY IS AT THE CORE OF THAT VALUE. THE BOARD SHOULD ENSURE THAT MANAGEMENT UNDERSTANDS IP AND HOW TO LEVERAGE THE CORPORATE VALUE OR PROTECT IT FROM COSTLY MISTAKES.

THERE ARE TWO PRINCIPAL ASPECTS TO INTELLECTUAL PROPERTY. THE FIRST IS CREATING AND SECURING OPPORTUNITIES. THERE ARE MANY OPPORTUNITIES IN ANY BUSINESS TO INCREASE PROFITS AND VALUE IF THE COMPANY HAS UTILIZED IP LAWS PROPERLY. AFTER A PATENT OR COPYRIGHT HAS BEEN GRANTED, PRODUCTS MUST BE PROTECTED FROM COPYING, LICENSES CAN BE GRANTED TO BUILD SALES, OR INVESTORS CAN INVEST BECAUSE THE ASSET THEY VALUE IS EXCLUSIVE TO THE COMPANY THAT OWNS THE IP.

> THE SECOND ASPECT IS SURVIVAL. INFRINGEMENT OF ANOTHER PERSON'S IP CAN BE DISASTROUS. IT IS NOT UNUSUAL FOR AN INFRINGEMENT SUIT DEFENSE TO COST HUNDREDS OF THOUSANDS OF DOLLARS AND MANY HOURS OF MANAGEMENT TIME. THERE IS A VERY REAL POSSIBILITY THAT A BUSINESS CAN BE SHUT DOWN IF IT LOSES AN INFRINGEMENT SUIT.
>
> JEFFREY SHELDON, MANAGING PARTNER, SHELDON, MAC & ANDERSON

VALUATION SUMMARY

Use the Sustainable Value Wheel as a model for creating the value you want from your company. Understand what strengthens each sector in the model. Develop a plan for each. Invest your attention, money, and resources in the areas that will yield the highest sustainable value.

Consider who would be interested in buying or investing in your company. Gather information on what parts of the Value Wheel they would value most highly. Use that intelligence to guide your value building efforts.

The next chapter will consider the next steps toward monetizing the value you and your company have created.

REAL COMPANY, NEW CEO

"I RECENTLY BECAME CEO OF A BUSINESS THAT HAD BEEN FAMILY OWNED FOR ALMOST FORTY YEARS. THE COMPANY HAD GROWN TO A SUCCESSFUL MID-SIZE COMPANY, BUT HAD ENCOUNTERED CHALLENGES. THE NEW ORGANIZATION REQUIRED NEW SKILLS AND EXPERIENCE ON THE BOARD THAT COULD WORK CLOSELY WITH A NEW MANAGEMENT TEAM TO GUIDE THE COMPANY. WITH MANY LONG-TERM RELATIONSHIPS BETWEEN THE FAMILY OWNERS AND BOARD MEMBERS, THIS WAS A DELICATE TRANSITION.

A FIRST STEP WAS AN ADVISORY BOARD MADE UP OF HIGHLY EXPERIENCED BUSINESS LEADERS. THEY WORKED CLOSELY WITH MANAGEMENT AND THE FAMILY OWNERS TO BOTH DEFINE THE FUTURE OF THE COMPANY AND THE GOVERNANCE APPROACH THAT WAS NEEDED. WE LEARNED ABOUT THEM AND THEY LEARNED ABOUT US, THE BUSINESS, AND THE FAMILY.

THE ADVISORY BOARD EVOLVED INTO A NEW FIDUCIARY BOARD COMPRISED OF FAMILY MEMBERS, TRUSTED INDUSTRY EXPERTS AND ADVISORY BOARD MEMBERS. THIS NEW FIDUCIARY BOARD HAS GREATLY IMPROVED THE GOVERNANCE OF THE COMPANY, INCREASED TRUST WITH AN OUTSIDE INVESTOR AND THE FAMILY AND ALLOWED FOR A SMOOTH TRANSITION FROM THE OLD FIDUCIARY BOARD."

RICH WHITE, CEO, FIRST REHABILITATION LIFE INSURANCE COMPANY OF AMERICA, GREAT NECK, NEW YORK

The Advisory Board Wants to Know:

1. How predictable are your future earnings, and what are the factors that may increase or decrease them?

2. How diverse is your customer base, and are these customers in different industries?

3. How diverse is your product line and service offering? Do they serve a variety of market segments?

4. Is your CEO highly bankable? Is that you? Would an investor believe the management team really could double the sales and earnings of this company in three years without you?

5. How strong is the infrastructure of the company? Can it be a platform that will support rapid, profitable growth?

6. Would a buyer be impressed with the culture in your company?

7. How strong is your gross margin, and what is the trend of this key factor?

8. Have you talked with an investment banker and a deal attorney to learn about the questions that come from due diligence and how you will answer them?

CHAPTER 8

End Game Options: In Play

"I made my money by selling too soon."
Bernard Berauch

We have now arrived at the last stage of play before this game ends. In the world of selling companies or attracting investors, you are ready to be "in play." Your company is ready to "go to market" if you choose to go there.

You have confronted the Five Challenges as described in Chapter One and you have:

1. *Survived*

2. *Built enough sustainable value so you have many choices*

3. *Created a process to consistently make good decisions*

4. *Gained alignment that led to effective execution*

5. *Defined your exit strategy and are in position to execute*

You have made the game-changing moves that give your company a higher level of sustainable value. You have the freedom to choose what you want to do and when you want to do it. Are you ready to start the process of selling the company? Or do you want to keep it and keep going? Or do you want to begin to transfer ownership to the next family generation?

This chapter shows options for transferring value and for creating a "liquidity event." A liquidity event is financial and legal code for selling all or part of your company. Your investment in your company will then be completely "liquid" if the sale terms are all cash.

Here is the overview of the process for getting to your end game in the next three years or earlier:

1. Decide that this is the right time for you to move toward your end game or to be "in play."

2. Engage in the professional advisory board process.

3. Clarify your definition of end game and timing with all owners.

4. Put your personal tax and legal houses in order.

5. Put your business tax, legal, and ownership houses in order.

6. Assess the options by getting outside professional input.

7. Decide on the terms of sale that are acceptable.

8. Create and commit to the plan and to the transaction team that will deliver the value you want.

9. Use the wisdom of the board and other professionals to avoid the problems and maximize the outcome.

TIMING

As the saying goes, "Timing is everything." The impetus to sell or change business ownership can come from external pressure, business challenges, or personal changes with the owner. You want this transaction to happen on your timing. If you can choose the right time for the market and for buyers, you have the greatest chance to realizing extraordinary results.

Valuations of most businesses have fluctuated as much as 75 percent up and down in the past five years. Outside influences have driven these changes more than internal factors. Over the past five years, money has been very easy or very hard to get. Investors have been attracted to industries or have run away from them. Private equity and corporate buyers have been active or have moved to the sidelines. ESOPs have been easy and inexpensive to fund or very expensive. Laws have changed. Yields on invested capital have risen and dropped.

The graph below demonstrates the importance of timing for company valuations and for monetizing sustainable value. It also shows the economic impact of the relationship between deals completed and multiples paid.

Historical U.S. **Middle Market M&A Activity**

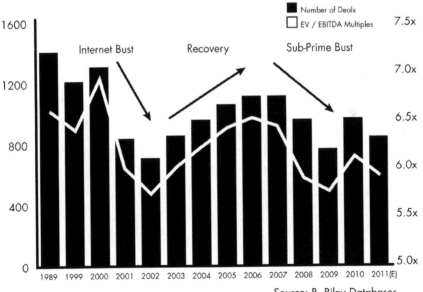

Source: B. Riley Databases

An important deliverable for a PABoard is assisting owners with the timing of a transaction by monitoring deal flow in the financial markets, financing availability, and buyer/investor appetites that are revealed in their investment banking networks.

The authors know of a case where the valuation of a company was defined by several outside buyers at over $100 million. The owners, the board, and the investment bankers moved as quickly as they could to get the transaction completed. Deal terms were discussed with the lead buyer. Then the buyer had a management change. The sale process stopped for three months. The market decline became apparent to all buyers during that three months. The buyer stopped buying. Two years later, the company was sold out of bankruptcy and the owners lost all their equity.

Owner's personal events and attitudes have tremendous impacts on timing. Owners and founders get tired of fighting the competitive and internal wars. People get sick. Financial pressures from banks and investors can force a sale of a business. Family members just want the money from the sale of the company—now. The owner may sell regardless of current market valuations, which could seriously lower the value of the transaction.

Owners should consider external and internal factors, but this is not a precise process. Through deliberation with the PABoard, the owner should look for clarity. If he can make a clear statement of intent, like the following, the process can move forward effectively: "My goal is to sell the company (or transfer to my children or my team) in X years. I would be satisfied with a net value of $Y million or more. Here are my non-negotiables around the terms of the sale. Let's put together the plan and the team and make it happen."

With that timing and value intention, the board, owners, and the transition team have a defined goal. Now all actions are measured against that schedule and valuation.

Time from Start to Close

How long does it take to complete a sale? There is no precise answer because a business is not sold or transferred until the buyer is ready to buy and the owner is ready to sell. That means that the value and the terms that the owner wants have been reached, legal hurdles have been overcome, and the owner is emotionally willing to sell to a qualified buyer who will meet the owner's terms.

The long time frame for delivering sustainable value could be two and a half to five years from the time that the value building process begins. This longer time frame is necessary if few of the critical valuation factors in the Sustainable Value Wheel are in place when a board forms. For instance, if the company has a low EBITDA, weak management team, and no strategic plan, it will take several years to put the changes in place and prove to a buyer that the changes are working.

If the critical factors are in place, the company is performing well, the owner is ready, and a willing and qualified buyer is identified, then a transaction could happen within six months.

Professional Advisory Board

The first step toward the transaction is to fully engage the advisory board. If the owners haven't formed an advisory board, they should create one. The owners need to be committed to the process that a professional board brings, be willing to endorse change, and be ready to deal with the "reality" of building sustainable value. Previous chapters describe the rudiments of selecting experienced professionals and beginning the process.

CLARIFYING OWNER'S END GAME

The next most important step is to clarify the owner's desire for building sustainable value and final monetization of their investment. Here are a few key questions:

- ❖ Are the owners really ready to transfer their business to a new owner?
- ❖ How much freedom do the owners want?
- ❖ What is enough in terms of purchase price or final distribution?
- ❖ Are the owners willing to agree to an earn-out over time?
- ❖ Are the owners and management willing to stay for a transition period? For how long, and under what terms?
- ❖ How will the owners respond to a new boss and a fiduciary board of directors?
- ❖ Can the owners tolerate a consolidation by the buyer or breakup of the company and subsequent dismissal of long-term employees?

PERSONAL TAX AND LEGAL PREPARATION

The owners must contact an estate attorney, a qualified tax accountant, and perhaps a wealth manager to design a plan that will maximize the amount he or she will keep after the transaction is complete.

Not only will the owners understand where they stand at that point, but they will learn how to structure their estate so that their wishes for the proceeds are managed. Finally, they will understand how to structure their assets and invest during the preparation period to minimize taxes and dispense proceeds effectively.

Don Natenstedt, Partner, Western Regional Manager of the accounting firm, McGladrey LLP, advises:

- ❖ *Do estate planning early before great value is created in the business.*

- ❖ *Gift ownership or cash while the business value is low.*

- ❖ *Create grandchildren's trusts.*

- ❖ *Keep enough to live on and enjoy, but set the tax structure so that the shareholders retain as much as possible when the company is sold or transferred.*

- ❖ *Set up a tax structure so that an equity partner can be added without a major tax impact.*

These changes in legal structure may not benefit the owner for years, so the sooner you implement them, the sooner the transaction can occur with the best payout retention.

BUSINESS TAX, LEGAL, AND OWNERSHIP STRUCTURES

Early in the process, talk to a "deal" lawyer, a "deal" accountant, and an investment banker. The goal is to have no legal or accounting issues and to have all the stockholders aligned with signed agreements in place. Then a sale can happen easily and fast. The price will also be higher because the buyer cannot say, "I would offer this price, *but* there are these legal problems, and your accounting is not

GAAP (Generally Accepted Accounting Principles) compliant, so I must offer less and hold some of the funds in escrow to cover my risk of problems after the sale."

One board confronted an accounting issue as the company prepared for sale. The company had a substantial inventory asset that was not easy to value. It had too many disparate pieces. The uncertainty of the inventory valuation clouded the value and had significant tax implications. The board recommended a sampling technique that the accountants and auditors approved. In year one, they conducted an outside inventory audit and came to an estimated value. In year two, they used the same sampling process and the value was about the same as year one. When the buyer and the IRS evaluated the sale, both agreed with the valuation process and the inventory value. The inventory valuation was no longer a stumbling block. The owners' tax bill lowered and there were fewer issues to overcome with the buyer.

Alignment of owners and the completion of shareholder documents such as buy/sell agreements, shareholder agreements, and voting rights are often areas for problems. Normalize these areas before any valuations are completed or buyer discussions start. Existing problems will magnify when the value of the shares becomes significant.

To gain trust in your financial statements and therefore higher transferred value, it is recommended that owners invest in audited financial statements by well-respected auditors. Reviewed financials may not be acceptable to many buyers or investors. Public companies may not buy your company until they have the certainty of audited financials. Most investors have the same requirement. The legal exposure for them is too high to trust financial statements that only a small accounting firm has reviewed.

GETTING YOUR HOUSE IN ORDER

Selling a business, like selling a house, takes work, and the process begins with a campaign to spruce things up.

The key is planning, up to and beyond the end game for maximizing the value you get from your business. This includes after-tax dollars, estate planning, and continued employment for employees, family members, or other shareholders. And, if you own the building you operate in, possibly includes a stream of income from a lease.

Many other factors are critical:

1. Setting goals based on a clear understanding of what the word "value" means to you and a potential acquirer or investor.
2. Getting professional management in place.
3. Obtaining audited financials.
4. Bringing order to all company records and contracts. Clean up the blemishes.
5. Obtaining top-flight help from investment banking, legal, accounting professionals, and your board.
6. Avoiding the million dollar mistakes like blown "S" Corporation Elections, incomplete corporate records, and failure to do thorough tax planning.

It takes time and money to get these elements in place. But the payoff is when you launch a campaign to sell your business, you will have already gone a long way toward establishing its real value and toward making the value credible to your potential buyers.

> LAWRENCE BRAUN, CHAIRMAN OF THE CORPORATE AND
> SECURITIES DEPARTMENT, SHEPPARD MULLIN, RICHTER &
> HAMPTON LLP

ASSESS THE OPTIONS

Owners have many options if they have created sustainable value and are following the process. Here are several options:

Retain and Build

Owners may wish to retain their business for future generations or improve the value while waiting for multiples to improve. The fundamentals described in Chapters Six and Seven should be instituted to keep improving value following this option. Owners should focus on the improvement of EBITDA, building the management team, and keeping their legal and financial houses in order. Advisory boards should support the shareholder's desire to grow, diversify, streamline, and add value to their business. Also, they should help build the management organization for the longer term to ensure effective succession plans.

This option also lends itself to growing through acquisitions and alliances. Owners should prepare an acquisition filter and a target roster for continuing review and evaluation. Acquisition filters vary, but some of the considerations are:

❖ Value-added components

❖ Enhancement of existing products and services

❖ Leverage of the distribution channels

❖ Accretive margins

❖ Internal rate of return improvements

❖ Technology that will yield a competitive advantage

❖ Improved service through geographic expansion

Sell Control

Owners may decide it is time to liquidate their holdings as a function of age, family concerns, desire to pursue another career, or merely to enjoy life from a new perspective. The end game is to transfer the highest value, gain freedom, and escape the owner's trap.

Strategic buyers or a private equity firm usually buy 100 percent of the stock or at least 51 percent. This event is called a majority equity recapitalization. Use the board to:

❖ Recommend, interview, and select an investment banker.

❖ Prepare for due diligence.

❖ Advise on employment contracts.

❖ Review valuation estimates.

❖ Evaluate letters of intent and purchase agreements.

❖ Coach the owners through the process.

Identifying potential buyers early can enhance sustainable value. Use your advisory board to help analyze them and make introductions.

Nurture the relationship with the buyer before you are ready for a transaction. Build the company the buyer would want if that is a good business strategy for you. Be ready to discuss a sale when the timing is good for you.

Moving a company from "industry average" to "extraordinary" valuations in the eyes of the investor or buyer creates significant wealth. As described in Chapter Seven, sustainable value comes when a company can demonstrate strength in the relevant sectors of the Sustainable Value Wheel.

Retain Partial Ownership

Private equity investors may be willing to purchase less than 50 percent of a company. This is a called a minority equity recapitalization. This transaction usually involves subordinated or junior notes with detachable warrants. The lender converts the ownership of the warrants into liquid value in one or two ways: piggyback registration rights if the company goes public or through a "put" that allows the company to buy back the stock.

Use the board to discuss the pros and cons of this path. There have been many happy marriages with this technique and some ugly separations and endings. One particularly ugly version of this option is the "loan to own" deal where the investor uses his contract to take over the company from the owner after only "loaning" money. This is a story that clearly illustrates this concept:

> One of the authors was looking for money to buy out his minority partners. Many investors said they would buy out the current partners, but that meant the author still had partners. Finally, one investor said, "I will loan you the money to buy out your partners. You will have 100 percent of the stock. I will not be your new equity partner. We will agree on the terms of principal and interest repayment; however, you cannot borrow from anyone else. If you miss one quarterly payment to me, I own the whole company." That is "loan to own" in its clearest, ugly form.

Going Public

The "going public" option becomes very interesting when there are large funding requirements to grow the business, and the level of company debt is near capacity. The owners should have clear reasons for going public and be able to answer the following:

❖ Is there a need to raise additional capital?

❖ Are there pending acquisition opportunities?

❖ Do we want to liquidate some of our holdings?

❖ Can we reposition the company with competitors and the financial community by being a public company?

❖ Are we willing to take on the aggravation and cost of meeting SEC regulations and public scrutiny?

After going public, the company must be able to attract investors and meet their expectations every quarter. The criterion for a successful public offering is often the company's ability to maintain strong revenue and profit growth. It must have a management team that is committed and capable, products or services that are interesting to investors, clear benefits of being a public company, and a receptive public stock market.

In this option, the owners must transition to a fiduciary board. Changing advisory board to fiduciary status is the best alternative because the PABoard members would know the company issues, opportunities, and its team. This knowledge would benefit the IPO (Initial Public Offering) by ensuring:

❖ A deep, capable management team

❖ A track record of successful, measured performance

❖ Sustained positive public image

❖ Clean, audited financial statements

❖ A transaction team of legal and accounting firms that is appropriate for the company's specific requirements

❖ The best underwriters

❖ Efficient and complete SEC S-1 registration process

❖ Professional and impactful "road show" for institutional buyers

Employee Stock Ownership Plans (ESOP)

Many owners are considering selling their companies to their employees through an ESOP transaction. There are several entities involved and the transactions between them are highly regulated in compliance with ESOP tax and fiduciary requirements.

ESOP Relationship Chart

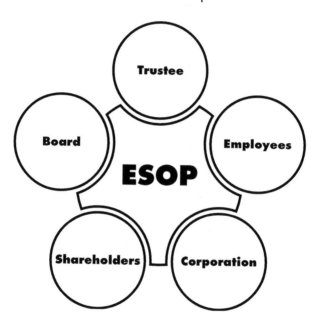

Anthony Mathews, Director of The Beyster Institute at the Rady School of Management at University of California at San Diego offers these ideas about ESOPs:

"ESOP transactions are more prevalent when interest rates are low. Banks have now had enough experience with this transaction, and the legal community has defined the risks for a company and the lender, so banks are now more likely to fund this vehicle.

An ESOP provides a process for a company to create liquidity for its owners while establishing a meaningful retirement benefit for employees. The ESOP is exempt from the diversification requirement applicable to other types of retirement plans and, in fact, is required to invest primarily in stock of the company that sponsors it. It can be funded by:

❖ Direct contributions of stock

❖ Cash contributions that are used to purchase stock from owners of the company

❖ Cash contributions that are applied to repay loans that were used to purchase larger blocks of shares. These can be funded with direct contributions which are subject to annual limits.

The sponsoring company receives tax deductions related to all contributions to the ESOP. This allows financing of stock purchases with completely tax deductible dollars (whether applied by the ESOP Trustees to principal or interest on ESOP loans).

Where ESOP ownership combines with a participative style of management that engages employees in the operation of the company, research shows the company will be more profitable and will grow faster. The company will have more loyal and productive employees, and, in return, those employees will accrue about three times the retirement benefits they would expect to find in other circumstances. Because of their significant tax benefits, their effect on the success of the sponsoring company, their impact on attitudes and actions of employees, and their ability to bring all those features into corporate transactions, ESOPs can play a meaningful role in a variety of corporate activities."

Leveraged Buy Out

Here the management team buys the company from the owners. The team usually invests about 20 percent of the price with their personal funds. The rest of the purchase comes from borrowed money or from extended terms from the owners. This strategy adds the burden of debt to the business, but the advantage is the business has a dedicated and knowledgeable management team who is highly incentivized to ensure that the business is successful.

Transfer to the Next Generation

Transferring value to the next generation involves all the moving parts we have addressed so far plus it has the added complications of the family's business and personal needs. The owner who transfers the value—probably the founder—also must live with the results and face the next generation owners often.

Transferring the family business is a dangerous undertaking. Fewer than 50 percent of family businesses survive under the leadership of the second generation according to John L. Ward in his book, *Perpetuating the Family Business*. He continues, "Only about 20 percent of family businesses last beyond sixty years in the same family."

The authors' experiences in private, non-family-owned businesses have paralleled those of Mr. Ward's work with family-owned businesses. All the principals for building sustainable value in this book apply to family-owned businesses.

CHALLENGES WITH FAMILY-OWNED BUSINESS VALUE BUILDING

The three most frequent areas for disagreement and mistrust among family ownership are open, honest, and clear communication; agreement on the distribution of earnings; and family member roles in the business. Families can manage these potential problems and other areas of misalignment by building basic governance structures and processes, such as:

❖ **A functioning and effective family council process.** *It enables the family members to define and guide the families' values, attitudes, commitments, and responsibilities toward the business. The process gains agreement on the family's continuing investment in the business and provides a forum for settling family disputes. It also can develop one voice from the family to the management team so that the team knows what is expected.*

❖ **Planning processes that span generations of owners.** *These long-term visions and strategies should be a competitive advantage to the business and a unifying process for the family.*

❖ **Family ownership structures that support the efficient operation of the family and the company.** *Here the family defines how to perpetuate ownership without creating problems and dysfunction. If the ownership structure is aligned, then the family and the company have a better chance of agreeing on how to build long-term, sustainable value for the next generations.*

Some important family questions to address are:

Does the next generation really want to own the company, or does it want to sell it after the founder leaves?

Is the answer to the first question unanimous or is there disagreement? If some, but not all of the family members want to sell their shares, how can that be accomplished?

Are there highly capable and committed family members who will run the business for the long term? If not, who will run it for the family, and what will the family's role become?

What is the family's policy on reinvestment in the business? Will they invest in growth or will they take greater dividends?

There are professional organizations that specialize in family-owned businesses. The authors recommend connecting with several listed in Appendix F. These organizations help families with the processes and structures that can support family owners as they wrestle with the dual challenges of managing the family and leading a successful company.

DETERMINE AN ACCEPTABLE SELLING PRICE AND TERMS

For most owners, it is very difficult to define the price and terms under which they will sell their company. This decision is as much emotional as it is numeric. The steps are:

1. *Select the appropriate transaction option.*

2. *Clearly layout the timing.*

3. *Establish the price range and terms the owners are willing to consider.*

4. *Agree on the non-negotiables, such as the lowest price or the worst terms or cultural fit.*

5. *Determine the trade-offs between your objectives and what a buyer/investor may be willing to concede—in not only purchase price but cash up front and holdbacks.*

Owners always get a dose of reality in this process. What they think the company is worth and what a buyer/investor will be willing to pay after due diligence may be very different. Use the advisory board and the investment banker to develop a valuation strategy and to identify, verify, and articulate the reasons why the company is worth the asking price.

Remember, the company needs to match its valuation drivers to the needs of the buyer/investor. The buyer will perform a lengthy and exhaustive due diligence process, but in the final analysis, the buyer usually has one to three strategic imperatives that drive the investment decision.

Price justification usually starts around industry financial comparatives, such as multiples paid in your market, EBITDA growth, quality of earnings, cash flow projections, and non-financial factors.

Prepare a list of value factors as described in Chapter Seven that can be addressed and tied into your valuation proposition. The following is a general list of questions to answer and to be ready to discuss with a buyer:

1. Does the company have a proven, sustainable business model?
2. Is there a unique selling/value proposition?
3. Will the company's information system drive operational leadership?
4. Are there favorable industry dynamics?
5. Is the company a market leader?
6. Does the company maintain a loyal, broad customer base?
7. Is there perceived brand equity?
8. Are there recurring revenue streams?
9. Does the company have multiple product lines?
10. Is the company a platform for acquisitions?

11. Can the company prosper without the founder?

12. Can the gross margin be sustained or grown?

Remember the old saying, "You can name the price if I can name the terms." A buyer may agree to your $50 million price, but pay half now and half if the company makes earnings targets after the sale. Or they may offer $50 million with 70 percent in cash and 30 percent in stock of the acquirer. Terms vary, but "it ain't cash until its cash." If you accept a portion of your sale price in future payment, do that only if the cash portion of the price is enough to satisfy you. If the second payout does not come, you will still have enough.

IRRATIONAL, HIGH PURCHASE PRICES

There can be a valuable wild card in this selling process. Buyers and investors sometimes become highly emotional and pay high prices that the financial people cannot justify. The most common driver of those irrational prices is auction fever for a "got to have" company.

One of the primary jobs of the investment banker is to create a perceived auction of at least two highly qualified buyers who do not want the other to get your company. The best driver of that irrational price would be at least two qualified bidders who consider your company a "must have" company.

Here is a model that maps the emotional purchase price:

Emotional Purchase Price

Buyers' Egos

Strategic Growth Opportunities

Management Team

Emotional Pricing   Value Escalators

Logical Pricing   Evaluation Standards

Financial Results

Industry Comparables

Lack of Problems

The authors were involved in one transaction where the owner had defined his walk-away deal as $32 million net enterprise value—all cash. This value equaled a 10x multiple of his $3.2 million in EBITDA.

Using an investment banker, the owner offered his company to the four industry leaders as a strategy enhancing acquisition. Each potential bidder knew the other three were bidding. The bidding opened at $32 million. Three bidders let the investment banker know they would bid up to $38 million. The bidding rose to $38 million and then to $45 million over a week of tense calls. At $50 million there were still two bidders: the industry leader, who was a public company with a high P/E (stock price divided by annual earnings) multiple and the number two company, a privately-owned company.

When the industry leader learned that number two was still bidding, he berated the investment banker, "You tell that owner that

I am putting $54 million on the table! Take that company off the market. I own it!" The investment banker, the owners, and the board conferred. We were happy to comply with his wishes *and* his $54 million cash offer.

RATIONAL

The winning bidder paid what appeared to the owners to be an irrational sum, but he had his rational reasons:

❖ He was in a "must win" state of mind because number two had bested him on three other deals.

❖ His company had a 35 P/E ratio. The price he paid was 17x earnings, which was more than twice sales. That was irrational to the seller, but it was better than the 35 P/E ratio on his public stock. The deal was accretive to his P/E valuation.

❖ He had committed to Wall Street that he would close two acquisitions that year. He closed this, his second acquisition of the year on December 31. Wall Street praised him.

LEARNING

Not all deals look rational to the seller. Be positioned for extraordinary value. Create auction fever between two or more buyers.

PREPARE THE PLAN AND BUILD THE TRANSACTION TEAM

Your transaction team will need at least the 6 disciplines shown in this model. The people on this team will often have conflicting priorities and guidance for you as they try to guide and protect you while maximizing the final outcome. In the end, you will have to make the final choices.

Transaction Team

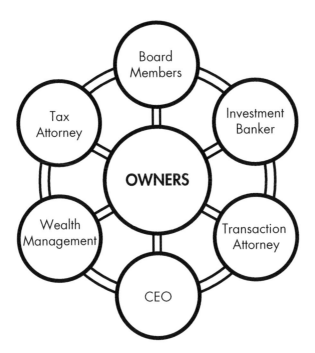

Once the owners have selected an option, they must prepare. If the owners decide to pursue a sale, here are several basic steps:

1. With the advisory board's guidance, select your deal accountant, deal attorney, and tax advisor. These professionals are usually not the current corporate advisors. They specialize in selling transactions and create value by doing what is needed to complete a transaction.

2. Interview and select an investment banker. It is imperative that you get the best assistance on negotiating strategy, valuation, and deal execution. These people can literally double the value of the transaction through their skills, knowledge, and style. Appendix G shows one company's set of criteria for investment banker selection.

3. Develop a checklist of all the issues and impediments that need to be addressed and will likely be reviewed in the due diligence process.

4. Normalize the financials by preparing a three-year pro forma of the results without the owner's expenses. Prepare the statements as if a strategic buyer or equity investor were to manage the business. Use your deal accountant and investment banker's expertise in this work.

5. Get the business's physical appearance in order. Do you need cosmetic alterations and clean up to make the premises attractive and professional?

6. An acquirer will review everything you have put into writing. Ensure that you and your advisors are comfortable with the information that is stored in your e-mail content, blogs, websites and all other written documents.

7. Identify the skeletons in the closet before they are discovered in due diligence by the buyer. Be prepared to mitigate the problems. Some skeletons that can reduce value are:

   ❖ Unusual bonus arrangements

   ❖ Equity promises

   ❖ Legal claims

   ❖ Environmental problems

   ❖ Intellectual property disputes

   ❖ Governmental investigations

8. Update your list of possible buyers/investors, both strategic and equity. Match your value propositions with the motivations of a likely strategic buyer or equity investor.

9. If you decide to go public, the owners need to identify and select underwriters that have experience in the company's market space. The advisory board will recommend possible candidates and firms.

10. Prepare a CEO white paper or executive summary on the industry and company. It crystallizes the value proposition and is a prelude to a "teaser" or selling document.

11. Develop and adhere to a structured selling process. Even if a transaction is not consummated with the first buyer, the company has already been greatly improved by doing the work to present itself. Timing is always the unknown in consummating a transaction. If the sale does not close because of a buyer's timing, remain connected, and as they say in basketball parlance, "stay near the hoop." Often, potential transactions that fall out can be reignited, or a new suitor may enter the picture. This is a process, not an event. It takes patience, a lot of guidance from the team, and a little bit of luck.

Principles for Negotiating a Sale

The authors have been involved in many sales. No two follow the same paths, but there are several general principles that are common to most successful transactions:

1. Do your own due diligence. Know the buyer or investor.

2. Be believable but firm at the beginning.

3. Be positive and unyielding on what is important to you.

4. Identify what is not important to you. Use these points to give in to show flexibility.

5. Have as many choices as possible, starting with at least two buyers.

6. Have the knowledge of what is realistic and doable.

7. Be persistent but calm and patient.

8. Listen a lot. Ask pertinent questions.

9. Always try to understand the buyer's motivation and position.

10. Build your strategy on well-defined strengths.

11. Drive your value proposition in all discussions.

12. Have a simplified list of key benefits of owning or investing in your company.

13. Do not sell the company yourself. Use a strong investment banker or lawyer to broker the deal.

DUE DILIGENCE...BE PREPARED

For owners, due diligence can be one of the most painful experiences of your life. It is the process used by the buyer to eliminate any risk in the transaction. It is also used to find reasons to reduce the purchase price or to change the purchase terms.

Everything that you have done, said, or written in your business will be scrutinized. The typical list of information requested will be at least three pages long and written in small print. Ask your deal attorney for a typical list.

Prepare for due diligence by conducting "mock" due diligence sessions with your management and advisory teams. Get input from your advisory board on what to expect.

While data rooms make the retrieval of data relatively easy, you and your team will have to gather all the data and documents. It will take weeks of work by a team of accountants, your employees, the investment banker, and your attorney.

Be sure to read the Representations and Warranties in your selling agreement. It will refer to the information you presented during the due diligence activities. These are the guarantees that you give the buyer about the information you have provided. If there are any problems with the company after the buyer has taken possession, this is the section of your agreement that can open the door for legal action by the buyer.

ON YOUR MARK! GET SET!

Moving through the selling process will be a very challenging part of your journey toward realizing the extraordinary sustainable value in your company. You will be on an emotional roller coaster. Sitting next to you will be your board, your family, and your transaction team. Long-term relationships will end. If the transaction is completed, you will be free.

The Advisory Board Wants to Know:

1. Are the owners emotionally ready for a transfer of ownership? Have the owners addressed the key questions about going forward?

2. Have you built your team of the best deal attorneys, accountants, and investment bankers? What do they advise?

3. Have the options been vetted with all of the owners and the PABoard?

4. Are all the owners' price and deal terms agreed upon and realistic?

5. Is there a true commitment to cope with the due diligence process?

6. Is the management team committed to the transaction?

7. Are you ready to do something else with your life? Are you excited about that next chapter?

Part IV

Completing Your End Game

CHAPTER 9

Your Commitment to Finish the Game

"Do not wait; the time will never be 'just right.' Start where you stand, and work with whatever tools you may have at your command. Better tools will be found as you go along."

George Herbert, British Poet, 1593-1633

The first eight chapters have focused on *how* to create sustainable value. If you follow the principles, you may have the freedom to transfer your company through a sale or keep it and enjoy it. It will be your choice.

But, remember, eventually, every company is sold to the next owner.

INVESTMENT BANKER, DENVER, COLORADO

AFTER SIX MONTHS OF WORK BY US AND THE COMPANY AND $100,000 IN EXPENSES, WE WERE FINALLY AT THE CLOSING. THE DOCUMENTS WERE ON THE TABLE FOR SIGNING. THE BANK ACCOUNTS WERE OPEN AND THE WIRE TRANSFERS FOR $48 MILLION WERE READY. THE OWNER WALKED INTO THE ROOM, SAW THE DOCUMENTS, TURNED PALE, AND LEFT. HE WAS NOT READY. NO DEAL. EVERYONE LOST. WE LOST OVER $1 MILLION IN FEES.

THE OWNER SOLD TWO YEARS LATER FOR $29 MILLION.

If you chose to move towards the exit now, will you be prepared to stay the course through to a sale?

The authors have spent twenty years observing and coaching the "exotic animals" know as owners of private businesses. Each one is different. There is no one answer to these questions: Why sell? Why now? Why this price? But, there are some common themes.

WHY OWNERS DO NOT SELL...NOW

The most common reason today for not selling is that the business is not worth enough. "I make more money with my take home pay from the business than I could if I had $20 million in the bank." If this statement (or one like it) is true, your current income is the top priority for you. If your company has good prospects, then do not pursue a sale. Wait until you feel the value will meet your income and security needs.

There are other reasons not to sell now. You are your business. You introduce yourself as, "I am Fred Schmidt. I am the Owner and CEO of Schmidt International." At your business, you have more power and control than in any other part of your life. Your business card affirms who you are. It is hard to leave that.

In the community, people honor the position of owner. Many of your friends are also business owners, vendors, bankers, or community organizers. You belong to the same clubs and organizations. How will they see you after you sell?

Selling will affect your spouse's life. Does your wife want to be seen as a retired person? She may enjoy the status of being a company owner. Maybe she married you "for life, but not for lunch every day," and she is not thrilled that you will be in her daily routine.

Without that label of "CEO," who are you? Who would care?

For these and many other reasons, owners often do not sell or transfer the company to the next family generation until they have to. They run their companies as long as they can and enjoy it.

Why Some Owners Do Sell

But, some owners do sell. Why? The bottom line is that their life after the sale looks better to them than the one they currently lead.

"Shake-Up" Events May Lead to a Sale

Often outside events wake up owners to other parts of themselves or to the world around them. Events the authors have seen are:

- ❖ *Health issues like a heart attack or some event that pulls you away from the business for more than a few weeks*
- ❖ *Death of someone close to you*
- ❖ *Change in an industry that stops long-term value building*
- ❖ *A lawsuit that takes away cash and freedom*
- ❖ *A divorce or a marriage*
- ❖ *Religious experiences*
- ❖ *A buyer's unsolicited offer that is very attractive*
- ❖ *A friend who sold for a lot of money and is living the good life*

When one of these events occurs, your priorities may shift. You could become dissatisfied with the prospect of spending the next ten years running your business.

Slower Changes in Awareness

For some, there is no shake-up event. There may be a series of small events or an awareness of time and aging. Owners have given these reasons for selling:

- ❖ I could have sold my business for $75 million three years ago. Next time things are strong and prices are higher, I am going to be ready to let it go.

- ❖ I just do not have the passion for my business that I had. I am tired of it.

- ❖ The future does not look very appealing. Government is everywhere. I should move out in the next few years.

- ❖ I have a strong calling to serve others. If I sell, I can really do something meaningful in my church or synagogue or community.

- ❖ My business partner wants to retire. I would not enjoy this business if he or she were not in it with me.

- ❖ I want to explore my spiritual questions.

- ❖ My daughter wants to become CEO someday and I am blocking her growth.

- ❖ I love to travel. I want to see the world while I can.

These and other influences may change your priorities over time. You may reach a tipping point when you know you are *really* ready to leave.

How Do I Think About Selling?

Larry Wilson, teacher and author of *Playing to Win!*, taught an old formula for making a commitment to change.

Decision Model

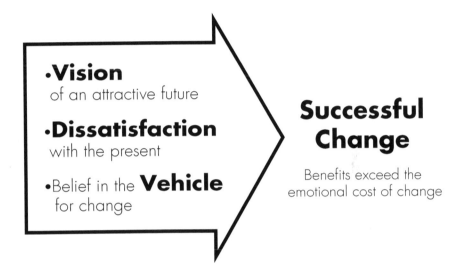

•**Vision**
of an attractive future

•**Dissatisfaction**
with the present

•Belief in the **Vehicle**
for change

Successful Change

Benefits exceed the emotional cost of change

Here is how this model works for any decision you want to make and how you can use it to consider selling your business:

Vision: Do you have a picture of what you really want to do or become outside of business? If you had the freedom to do it, would you? Are you excited about it?

Dissatisfaction: Are you highly dissatisfied with running your company? Is it not meaningful or interesting? How badly do you want to be out of your business role? See "shake-up" events above. How is your health?

Vehicle for Change: Is selling the business the best vehicle for change? Do you believe that you could get the freedom you want if you sold your business? Or, is it better to change your role in the company to gain what you want?

Cost of Change: Everything costs something. When you think through those costs, are they worth it to achieve your vision? How would it feel to be a former owner? Would it be a successful change?

Judy Swayne, Founder and Executive Director of the Orange County Community Foundation relayed this story about her decision to retire. An advisor asked her these four questions:

1. With what you have done at the enterprise, have you satisfied your need for a personal sense of accomplishment?

2. Has the enterprise accomplished what you wanted it to accomplish?

3. If there is more for this enterprise to do, do you have the energy, desire, and ability to take the organization to a new level?

4. Are you missing important things in your life because of your commitment to the enterprise?

A related question was added by Pete Lakey, a respected Vistage chairman and coach, "If there is still more to do to reach your dream, do you have to do it, or will others carry it forward for you?"

SHORT STORIES OF THOSE WHO HAVE SOLD

Owners who have sold find a wide variety of things to do after they sell. They become different people. They often live out dreams they had set aside while running their companies. Their card no longer says "CEO" but something totally different. Here is what a few owners did:

❖ She and her husband moved to Hawaii. They live there on a large farm overlooking the ocean. They grow fruit trees. They delight in the sound of the whales that migrate near their shores.

She is active in a regional non-profit organization that serves inner-city kids, and she runs the farm. He teaches, writes, and works to change the American system of education.

❖ This CEO tried board work and creating a single-digit golf handicap after he sold. He helped his children and grandchildren. He decided his passion was working in business to solve problems. He joined a private equity group and is now the non-executive chairman of a $1 billion, international firm. He is having a great time while his wife is chairperson of several non-profit boards. They both spend a lot of time with the family and their church.

❖ After he sold his business, he started a rock band and set up a shelter for damaged pit bulls. He travels and still advises the owners of the business he sold. He likes to invest in start-ups and younger entrepreneurs.

❖ She now travels the world with a culinary group and works with a large charity that helps third world countries. She remodeled her home, and it is remarkable. Her priorities are exploring who she is, and exploring her place in the universe.

❖ He spent several years after his heart attack with an organization that restores hearts through diet, stress reduction, and exercise. He came back 100 percent. Now he is certified as a search and rescue professional. Saving people is a meaningful part of his life.

❖ He did very little differently after he sold. Lives in the same house. Has the same friends. He travels more with his wife, plays golf, and serves on several boards. He actively invests his proceeds in real estate and other diverse vehicles.

❖ After he sold, he added several buildings to his holdings. He has a team to manage his real estate, but he is passionate about doing the deals. He collects unusual cars. He and his wife travel the world buying and sometimes selling cars and connecting with fellow collectors. They really enjoy their children and their dogs.

❖ This person became a consultant and a bridge CEO for companies shortly after selling. He leads workshops for CEO groups, coaches owners, serves on boards, and is writing a book. He and his partner work a day a week to support a local nursing home. Children and grandchildren are important in their lives.

THE FREEDOM OF SUSTAINABLE VALUE

There are many ways to live and many things to do when you let go of the day-to-day operations of your company. By creating sustainable value, you have the means and the freedom to keep, sell, or transfer your company.

Make your choice and move with conviction. Enjoy your best life.

THE PABOARD'S ROLE IN THE SELL DECISION

The PABoard should be neutral and independent when it helps the owner deal with the question of selling. It should look at the state of the business and the industry, the ability and energy of the owner, the will of the shareholders, the strength of the balance sheet, and many other factors.

If the board feels that the company should prepare for sale, they will recommend it. If the owner puts the sale issue on the agenda, then the board should conduct a impartial review to determine what actions will yield the best outcome for the owner, his family, the shareholders, and the company.

The Advisory Board Wants to Know:

Now that you know what it takes to create sustainable value and you have considered the alternatives and their costs, what end game do you want to commit to? Your PABoard should ask you the following:

1. Do you have the energy and passion to grow the business and push the changes needed to get to the vision you want or need for this business?

2. Do you have the needed skills, or does the company need a new CEO to build the sustainable value you want?

3. If you were not running this business, what would you be doing? How passionate are you about doing this? Is it meaningful for you?

4. What proceeds do you need from a sale in order to feel safe? What income is enough so that you have the freedom to do what you want?

5. If selling your business means losing contact with the people you work with and with some of your business associates, how much does that matter?

6. If there are other shareholders, are you and they aligned on selling the company?

7. What does your spouse or most trusted advisor say about selling?

8. What is your decision?

CHAPTER 10

Rules of the Road to Freedom

"Almost anything can be achieved in small, deliberate steps. But there are times you need the courage to take a great leap; you can't cross a chasm in two small jumps."

David Lloyd George

If you decide to sell, here are a few closing "rules of the road" gained from many transactions:

❖ Manage the company as if you're going to sell it so you can when the opportunity arises. Always be building something valuable.

❖ Follow the guidelines for building sustainable value as shown in the Sustainable Value Wheel. They build options and freedom for owners and their companies.

❖ Identify and nurture target buyers and investors early.

❖ Identify and connect with a transaction team well before you actually need them.

❖ Build a valuation map to drive extraordinary multiples.

❖ Be prepared for a dose of reality. Valuations often do not meet owner's expectations.

❖ Get as much cash up front as you can if you sell. Earn outs and seller's notes are usually not paid in full.

❖ If you choose to sell and stay, have a top-flight attorney negotiate your employment agreement.

❖ Your buyer may offer to let you reinvest in the newly structured company. Do not reinvest in the deal unless you have a graduated recovery of your investment if you leave involuntarily. Evaluate all the risks with the help of your advisory board.

❖ Update your estate plan and have pre-determined investment alternatives for the proceeds.

❖ Understand buyers/investors motivations. Where are they taking the company? What changes are they likely to make? How will these changes affect the owners, financially and emotionally?

❖ Before and after the deal consummation, build a paper trail from the meetings with the buyers. If it isn't in writing, it often doesn't happen. You cannot predict human behavior.

❖ Always introduce competition. It modifies behavior. One buyer is no buyer, and it is not an auction.

❖ Do not give up control unless the shareholders are completely satisfied with the cash payout and will be willing to walk.

❖ Beware of "loan to own" scenarios.

❖ Remember, everyone has an agenda—everyone.

❖ Loyalty too early comes at a high price.

❖ Buyers/investors value predictable earnings. They can hold shareholders hostage to what was represented as future results.

❖ Beware of the representations and warranties in your selling, as they will be used against you.

❖ Everyone needs to know where the exit is.

❖ Be ready to live a life beyond your business.

❖ Be patient. This may take years.

❖ Remember the people who got you there. Share.

| The Advisory Board Wants to Know: |

Buckle your executive seat belt. You are in for an amazing ride!

1. How can your board members help?

2. Where are you going to spend your time for the six months after the sale closes?

3. What are you going to do to celebrate?

4. If there is no sale, what is plan B?

Chapter 11

How Real Owners Played Their Board Game

The authors have had the privilege of being involved with many owners who created significant sustainable value using the professional advisory board process. Here are some of their stories.

Strawberry Fields Forever: Growth Through Acquisition

Sunrise Growers and Frozsun Foods are based upon a vertically integrated business model in the fruit and vegetable space, processing fresh and frozen foods from field to fork.

We developed an advisory board primarily to manage a growth strategy through acquisitions. We assembled a seasoned group of experienced board members who provided different skill sets, yet could act as a team to support growth and provide the financing necessary to fund the strategy.

With a well-designed plan, the senior management team was able to grow the business from $100 million to $300 million in sales through six significant acquisitions. We were then able to conduct and evaluate how to achieve a liquidity event through taking the company to market and, ultimately, completed a private transaction with an East Coast private equity firm.

Our advisory board was invaluable in the entire process, including providing guidance on working with the new private equity owners. The transition from privately-owned to professionally-managed ownership was greatly enhanced by the board's input. Our board of advisors was the key to our firm's double-digit growth and, specifically, my development as a CEO during this period.

My advice to business owners is that you cannot afford *not* to have a board of experienced advisors who provide objective business advice and to be a thought partner for the CEO.

Doug Circle, Founder and former CEO of Sunrise Growers and Frozsun Foods

Four Generations of Containers

I am the fourth generation in my family's wholesale distribution business. I decided to form a board of advisors for two main reasons: to provide a resource for my wife (who is not active in the business) in the event of my death or incapacity and to provide outside perspective and experience in helping me make key strategic decisions.

My board consists of four people I have known and trusted for a long time: an attorney, a CPA (not the company's CPA), a seasoned businessman and consultant, and an experienced former owner of a business in my industry. The balance and camaraderie on the board has been so good that I have not changed the composition in almost twenty years.

The first issue where I needed the board's help was how to confront a non-performing *key* employee. I was avoiding making the necessary decision, and it was hurting the company. The board's advice was brutally correct. They asked me, "Would you like your epitaph to read 'He was good to his *key employee*, but he lost the company?'" The board helped me to prepare for the inevitable confrontation and to develop a fair severance package.

The board also played a critical role when the company faced a financial crisis. I had borrowed a considerable sum to build a plant. Several unexpected setbacks put us out of covenant with our bank with potentially devastating consequences. This was my first experience with the pitfalls of being overly leveraged, and I was in a panic. My decision-making ability was clouded by my fear of failure. Several members of my board had gone through a similar challenge. They helped me develop a recovery plan and make a confident presentation to my bank. The bank agreed to a covenant waiver. We were back in covenant within six months (after some significant cost cutting).

Although I have always been a good strategist, idea person, and leader, I am not always the best day-to-day manager. My board recognized this, but had a very hard time convincing me to hire a COO to handle the daily management of the company. After a series of managing frustrations, I was finally ready. With the board's help, we conducted a search and hired a COO. To my surprise, I selected one of my board members (the industry insider). We have been working together for five years now, and it is one of the better management decisions I have made.

Jeff Levine, former Chairman and CEO of United States Container Corporation

Metagenics: Grow the CEO, Grow the Company

Metagenics was a small (approximately $50 million), yet rapidly growing company. We were considering an equity transaction

(IPO or private equity) to help us finance future growth and possible acquisitions.

As an entrepreneur, founder, and CEO, I wanted to learn how to function under a board of directors and wanted to tap the expertise of senior executives who had already been through what I was considering for our company. The advisory board option was a perfect fit for our company and me. It was very helpful to me in navigating a variety of difficult challenges, three acquisitions, and two financings while growing the company to revenue over $240 million.

Working with one of the authors of this book, John Zaepfel, I interviewed advisory board candidates and selected experience sets and personalities that I thought would be good fits for our business. Then we got to work. We met monthly for the first three months and then went to quarterly meetings. The board would ask probing questions that helped me better think through complicated issues and come to better decisions. The board interaction improved the depth of my thinking, and that carried over into the day-to-day decision making.

As an entrepreneur with many ideas, one of the most significant benefits of the board was helping me stay focused. They helped us focus on the most important opportunities and continued to improve the focus on our strategic plan. That focus helped us make faster and more profitable progress. They also provided guidance and insight into the financial management of the company, helping to improve profitability, guarding the integrity of the balance sheet, and managing the relationship with our auditors. Their guidance on organizational development was also helpful in reaching our goals.

Looking back, I feel that the most profound benefit of the advisory board was that it helped me grow my CEO skills and keep up with the changing demands of a growing company. It was a very good experience.

Jeff Katke, CEO, Metagenics

BOARD POWER—OWNER AND BOARD MEMBER PERSPECTIVE

I have experienced advisory boards from two perspectives. First, as owner/CEO of a rapidly growing privately-held company, I utilized an advisory board. Second, I have served as a member of a number of advisory boards. I have experienced the power of an advisory board as a beneficiary, as well as witnessed its impact as an advisory board member.

I believe that one of the most important things an advisory board does is help the owner determine and clarify the outcomes he wants and then hone them into objectives with well-delineated plans for their achievement.

The second thing an advisory board does to help create the outcomes the owners want is to provide an objective outside view of the company. Too often, the owner/CEO is too close to the business and the people in the business to assess strengths and weaknesses. Helping the owner see the company objectively through an experienced outsider's perspective is essential to achieving the desired outcomes.

Finally, advisory boards are typically composed of individuals with considerable business experience. The sharing of the lessons learned from their collective experience is invaluable in addressing issues and challenges as they arise.

It is clear to me that advisory boards can be tremendously impactful in helping owners achieve the outcomes they want, but they must be matched up with an owner/CEO who is open to challenging questions and insights and can translate these into a sustainable effort to realize the full benefit of an advisory board.

Keith Swayne, former owner and CEO of Case Swayne

FIRST TIME ENTREPRENEUR: *MPS* BOARD OF ADVISORS

I learned about advisory boards from my TEC (Vistage) chairman, Ann Ehringer. Ann suggested that I should get help from people who were professional, experienced in running companies, and knowledgeable about growing companies. I didn't need an accountant, banker, or lawyer on staff. I could contract with them as needed. Ann introduced me to Walt Sutton, Bill Hawfield, and John Nelson. All of them had experience well above mine. I was amazed when they agreed to come on the board. I never asked why, but I think one reason is that they wanted to give back what they had received.

We decided on quarterly meetings, for a half day. What I got out of the meetings was priceless. This was the first time I had owned my own business. It was hard to get honest opinions because everyone worked for me, which biased any input. Besides, they all thought I knew what I was doing.

In the board meetings, we all did not think alike, which was a wonderful luxury. I promised myself that I would listen to all sides and at least try what the board suggested. Before forming the board, it was easy to say no to things that I didn't want to do. After the board, it became not so easy. I had to commit to what to do, how to do it, and when to do it. The board followed up on the action plans we set.

The board members were always prepared when they showed up. I quickly learned that they truly cared about the company and me. Their advice, energy, and thoughts were all geared to my success, which also made me not want to disappoint them.

The board insisted I put together an end game and a strategic plan to get there. They pushed me to reinvent our business model from a job-shop model to a recurring revenue model. We moved from document scanning to document storage and became a document management company. It was an uncomfortable change. As we approached the end game period, I focused on the new model and put the plan in action with the board's help, input, and approval.

Based on lots of hard work, a good plan, a strong team, and the board's advice and support, the business grew beyond our expectations. Soon, the business was delivering almost 30 percent pretax profits while my competitors were struggling to get up to 10 percent, if they were profitable at all.

After three years of work, we sold the company at a multiple and dollar amount I had never dreamed of. To say I am a believer in boards of advisors is an understatement. I am living in Reno and skiing to my heart's content, thanks in part to my three board members.

Richard Ross, former owner and CEO of MPS, Inc.

SECURE SUCCESSION, REDUCE RISK, AND BUILD VALUE

When I bought out my partner, I became the only shareholder in the business. The risk of what could happen to the business in case

I'm not around and what that would mean to my family and my employees magnified.

My wife had very little exposure to the business. The concept of an advisory board initially became appealing to me as a succession plan and as a way to maximize the sustainable value of the business. Today, with an advisory board, my wife has a very capable group of advisors that will help her find a replacement and decide the future of the asset in case I am not around. It can evaluate candidates, choose a CEO, and develop a transition plan so the impact of my loss on the business would be minimal.

I also included my wife as an advisory board member so she would get to know the other members and build trust. She is an attorney by training, and in this process, she has become a contributing member of the board.

The board has become an important part my business. It helps me evaluate strategic options and set the course for the business.

More specifically, the board helped me evaluate and stop a high-risk, multi-million dollar IT platform project. We were fully committed to it, but the board helped me develop other options including licensing and a merger.

We also were strongly considering a merger. The board became actively involved and went as far as meeting the CEO of the company I was considering merging with. It provided feedback on the risks and rewards of the merger knowing our culture, the personalities, and the risks involved in the deal. They advised against the merger, and I ended the negotiations. The advisory board has also helped me evaluate investments in product development and real estate.

What makes them very helpful is that they have become familiar with my personality, my family, our company culture, my team, my strengths, and my weaknesses. They are able to give me open feedback from good understanding, caring, and with no hidden agendas.

My only regret is that I should have started it earlier.

Stan Megerdichian, President & CEO, Peak Performance

How Boards Add Shareholder Value

This is from the value creation perspective of an M&A advisor:

Boards add significant value to almost any privately held business, and in many ways. A few examples:

- *Boards help keep the shareholders focused and on the same page with regard to key, big-picture issues—company philosophy and culture, growth opportunities, strategic vision, financial and operational planning, plan execution, ongoing review of key performance indicators, management recruiting, development, compensation, and succession. This builds alignment and efficient execution.*

- *Boards assist in making management teams more clearly and objectively accountable to shareholders. The reverse is also true and is a very good idea, but it's of particular importance when heading into a sale process.*

- *Boards provide a critically needed dose of intellectual honesty between owners (particularly those who are active in management versus those who are passive/absentee, in control versus in the minority, and the older generation versus the younger).*

- *Boards can also act as a key "check and balance," acting if necessary as a referee in disagreements between owners and management team over strategic objectives, plans, and budgets.*

Are they reasonably attainable or overly ambitious, shortsighted or pie-in-the-sky, and are they likely to advance the company along its longer-term path and increase the value of the owner's equity?

Lars Ekstrom, Founder and Managing Director, Augeo Advisors, LLC

TWO CHEFS ON A ROLL: A RECIPE FOR SUCCESS

At the time that my business partner and I were researching the advantages of an advisory board, we had been in business for sixteen years. We were on a growth curve that brought many issues to the forefront and needed to make key decisions.

We were outgrowing our facility. We had not built the infrastructure to delegate many of the daily functions necessary to operate. We had not written a formal strategic plan nor formulated an exit plan.

The formation of an advisory board was instrumental in helping to bring focus into our business. One of the first discussions concentrated on how to grow to the next level and what our succession plan would be as we delegated control of the business. Out of this meeting, the board suggested we hire a president and build a top-notch executive team. We needed to find great people in finance, marketing and sales, operations, R&D, HR, and IT. The board members knew our industry and knew a lot people. They helped us recruit the game breakers that we needed in each position.

This team and the process allowed us to work toward a five-year decision point. We could plan growth. With a good strategic plan, we went to the banks in advance for financing.

Our advisory board consisted of five business people who had knowledge in financing, marketing, operations, and human resources. This mix of expertise was invaluable because they challenged our thought processes and our ability to meet our goals and expectations. They helped us to make tough decisions.

They were there for us throughout the years. In our twenty-third year of business, we were ready to exit on our terms. They helped us select an investment banker and a top-notch lawyer to take us through the successful sale of our company.

The proceeds from the sale were more than we expected. We were glad to share part of our proceeds with the management team that got us there and with the board of advisors who helped guide us.

Eliot Swartz, co-chairman, Two Chefs on a Roll

CRITICAL BOARD ROLE: CONSISTENTLY GOOD DECISIONS

From my experience as an independent member of the advisory boards of public and private companies and from coaching executives, it seems clear to me that the role of the outside advisor with inside information is crucial in helping owners and their executive teams make good decisions. These decisions must be consistent with their personal values (which inevitably drive the company) and with the essential elements of good decision making.

The owner/president's most important skill sets are those of self-awareness of his or her core values and personal principles, of what is takes to make good decisions consistent with those values and with their patterns of thinking, and of how to work well with and through the efforts of other people. The role of the advisor is to help the owner and his team to achieve and employ all those skills.

Entrepreneurs typically, and unconsciously, follow one of two patterns in making decisions—what I have called (see *MAKE UP YOUR MIND: Entrepreneurs Talk about Decision Making*, Merritt, 1995) one: "analysis confirmed by feeling" or two: "emotions supported by data."

A good decision includes both thorough analysis (doing the homework) and recognizing emotions (being aware of one's feelings about the possible or probable consequences of a decision, particularly its consistency with one's values). A decision that is based on both of those efforts (analysis and emotional awareness) is most apt to be a good decision; a decision that relies only on one or the other (analysis or emotion) is quite apt not to be.

It is one of the responsibilities of the independent board member to encourage decisions based on both of these efforts—to act as not only a sounding board but also as an accurate and objective mirror of these efforts by the executive(s) and the board. And, to say so in a manner, tone, and language that the board can hear and understand. That level of communication in itself is a learned skill for almost all board members.

It also is typical of most of us that we have a particular pattern to employing analysis and recognition of our emotions—first one and then the other. If we are aware of these personal thinking patterns, we will include both in our decision making and, therefore, make better decisions. An actively listening independent board member can be especially helpful in pointing out when shortcuts may be distorting the discussion process and may be instrumental in expanding the conversation and the considerations to include all sides of an issue.

ANN GRAHAM EHRINGER, PhD, Owner of Saddle Peak Lodge and board member of several private companies

OUTSIDE THINKING, INSIDE CULTURE AND SECURITY

When I decided to have an advisory board, I looked for a group of people who could bring my management team and me different ways to think about the complicated challenges we faced. I wanted and needed different and diverse opinions that we were not always able to come up with. We are a close-knit management team. There was the danger that we could be predictable in our thinking and miss possible alternatives or make wrong decisions.

I chose board members who were sophisticated and worthy of respect by our team. With that respect, the board could hold management accountable for the right decision processes and for following through on the actions committed to by my team. Each of the people we selected had strong but different skills and experiences. They each appreciated the Vistage process for conducting effective meetings. They knew when to ask questions, when to give advice and when to pull me "out of the weeds."

It was very important to me that these outside people understood my values and style. They needed to know the culture we have at IMS so they could give good advice that fit my culture, which is so precious to me. Service to our customers is the highest priority; being a great place to work is the second.

Another reason to have this board is to give my family and my employees the assurance that the company would run well if I were not in the picture. If something happens to me, the advisory board becomes our fiduciary board. It has clear instructions on the steps to take to ensure that my estate and family realize the highest value for the company and that our employees are treated fairly.

This board gives me the security that helps me sleep at little better. I could not imagine running my business without having this group of people as my sounding board.

Neil Sherman, Chairman and CEO of Industrial Metal Supply

TWO CHEFS AND A BOARD

Two Chefs on a Roll, was the first company to have chefs partner with customers to co-develop signature menu items and private-label retail products. My partner (who had also been cast in the role of my husband) and I built it up from a kitchen to a garage to a 100,000-square-foot facility, from just me to over 300 employees. The story of our advisory board is a tale of how partners get stuck and about how collaborations with experienced outsiders can make the impossible suddenly become possible.

After thirteen years of over 30 percent year-in, year-out growth at Two Chefs on a Roll, our unique, best-you-can-find-anywhere pastries, sauces, and dips business, were no longer on a roll.

We had hit a ceiling of knowledge—individually and as partners. One reason growth had stalled was miscommunication and paralysis. When my husband and I decided to divorce but continue as partners, we agreed that neither of us would make business decisions without the other. That was challenging.

Our pact meant that when he wanted to buy new equipment, I said, "No way," and when I wanted to go after new accounts or get involved in a professional organization, he said we couldn't afford it. Every time I brought back something new, he reacted as if I were trying to proselytize some deranged new religion. When growth went stagnant, we faced even bigger decisions that required us to come together.

We had finished our buy/sell agreement and reassured our bank, employees, and customers that nothing would change and that we were still rock-solid business partners. The fact was that we had morphed into Two Chefs, a Therapist, an Accountant, and an Attorney on a Roll. Something had to give.

A formal board of directors was unnecessary; what we needed was terrific, experienced, professional advice. My Vistage chair gave me a tape about advisory boards that talked about everything we deserved in a board.

My partner was right. We couldn't afford it, but we began learning not to see that as a stumbling block. I hired Bill Hawfield to help me, and together we figured out what we could offer to incredible board members (including superb take-home desserts). We conducted interviews and presented our board package to the candidates. We attracted a finance person, a CEO with deep marketing experience, and another CEO with a strong operations background. Now we had access to professionals with much more experience in critical areas than we had, (although not one of them could bake the kind of chocolate cake we could).

Sixty days later, we held our first meeting at my home to ensure we had complete privacy to discuss our challenges. After some embarrassing arguments in front of our brand-new illustrious advisors, my partner and I embraced the possibilities of what this group of talented individuals could bring to our business.

Two years into the process, my father, also a seasoned executive, joined our advisory board. This changed the group's dynamic, in part because my dad had a more personal involvement than other members and in part because he was a minority investor.

We had assembled outside experts to mediate and contribute to those tough conversations we hadn't been able to navigate alone. For instance, when discussing how much to spend on marketing, our finance advisor said, "I've been a CFO for several different companies, and each one has spent between this and this percentage on marketing." That was the credible information we needed, so we made the decision and acted on it.

The board was instrumental in getting us to hire a CEO. It had only taken two board meetings before one of our advisors said, in a not-so-calm voice after listening to the two of us bicker, "One of you has to sell out to the other, or you have to bring in somebody else to run this."

To reach our dreams, I knew our company needed a professional manager or CEO—someone experienced in complex management issues, who understood strategy and structure. And, I knew that we would need an expensive executive team. Going for the dream would require a huge commitment to growing, which meant continuing to take on risk—big risks—for a long time.

One reason why I had felt we needed a professional manager was that we increasingly found that my partner and I weren't able to spend our time on the things each of us was great at and loved. The advisors helped us get excited about the very real possibility of letting somebody else deal with employee challenges and the bank—all those issues that were making us individually miserable and miserable as a partnership. We had built that business up to where it was by knowing and using our individual strengths and passions. Now we could hope to get back to doing what we really enjoyed and what made us unique.

Hiring a CEO is something owners could hem and haw about for years. Some business owners can't wrap their minds around how it could possibly work. But, working with an outside recruiter and the board, we went through this astoundingly complex journey and created a job description, an incentive plan, and a commitment in four to five hours! The impossible was looking real and believable.

We hired the CEO, who one of the board members recommended. Within only six months, we had a plan the board approved, and we were on track for growth, with the clarity to achieve a dream we all shared. One of the most valuable things we learned through this amazing process was that, often, we both wanted the same things, but our ways of formulating our needs and intentions were worlds apart. The board process had very quickly brought us back into the same orbit.

Six years and many "bet the kitchen" decisions later, we had more than doubled our business, had a world-class executive team in place, and had stayed true to our advisory process. We ultimately sold the company for much more than we expected. With those profits and our new wealth of wisdom about how the impossible becomes reality, we set out to invent new roles for ourselves in new fairy tales.

Lori Daniel, co-chairman, Two Chefs on a Roll

BATTERIES AND A COMPANY THAT LASTS

Trojan Battery is an eighty-seven-year-old family owned business with a governing board made up entirely of family members. We felt an advisory board with outside members could provide a way for the owners to reach outside this family circle for a broad spectrum of knowledge and experience. We wanted to create a board that looked to the future, forcing ownership and management to consider challenges and opportunities ahead and react accordingly.

For the past twelve-plus years, we have utilized an advisory board made up of three outside advisors and four members of management. Because of their experience and knowledge, the management team has been challenged along the way in all phases of the business and been supported where needed when presenting key strategic opportunities to the outside shareholders.

With a lot of help from the advisory board, the company finds itself today moving in a new strategic direction. We are globally focused. The company operations are performing at a record level. And, we have a relatively new leadership team proving to be very capable of implementing this new strategy.

Rick Godber, Chairman and CEO of Trojan Battery

INSURANCE FOR A SMOOTH TRANSITION

As owners of a successful, third generation family-owned business, we decided to invest in significantly increasing the value of our business. We brought in several professional managers from larger companies. We also decided to enhance our governance structure with the addition of new board members who could help us manage our new management team and keep us on the path of growing our business.

As an interim step to changing our fiduciary board, we formed an advisory board. This allowed us and the potential new fiduciary board members to get to know us, each other and the company. They could better assess their risks and fit as board members. We could learn how they thought and what they added to our company. The new management team was pleased to see added talent and perspectives.

When we moved to attract an investor in our business, we found that the advisory board members had experience in this change and gave us good advice. The investor valued the level of governance from the advisory and fiduciary boards.

The investor became a shareholder. As part of the restructing, we moved several of the advisory board members on to the fiduciary board. They knew our business, the family members and the investor. The management team trusted them. The transition was smooth and effective.

I would recommend using an advisory board as a productive process even if an owner does not change his fiduciary board. And, it can be a very effective way for both owners and advisory board members to increase the chances of a good outcome when fiduciary boards are formed.

Dr. Seth Goldberg

Chairman of First Rehabilitation Life Insurance Company of America

Great Neck, New York

PRESERVING THE PRINCIPAL

We create educational materials for pre-school and K-1 teachers. My family and I rely on the board for clear insights on all aspects of how to continue to build a strong, valuable company. They work at a strategic as well as at a tactical level. For instance, when we had some tough negotiations with the bank, John Zaepfel and Brian Stone from our advisory board were invaluable resources. They knew what to expect, prepared the "lesson plan" for working with the bank, and guided me through to a successful outcome.

Jim Connelly, CEO of Creative Teaching Press and YPO Member

OUTSIDE-IN WISDOM

As CEOs and business owners, we tend to work *in* the business to make sure things run smoothly and that all the fires are kept to a minimum. We all want growth, profits, sustainability, and increased shareholder value, yet we seldom look outside the business at the external drivers that affect those desired outcomes.

We hired a PABoard at Filanc to help us look beyond the day to day and to identify what needs to be done to achieve all of our "wants". Our PABoard helps us find the clarity of what needs to be done beyond the "day to day" so that we can have our successes. Our Board's collective experience doubles the effective experience of our Executive Team at a fraction of the cost and brings real world experience to quality decision making. While preparing for and during our PABoard meetings, we get the benefit of time spent outside the business working *on* values drivers for the business. Oh, and we also learn something in the process!

Mark Filanc, Chairman and CEO, Filanc Construction

APPENDICES

Appendix A
Sustainable Value: Board Discipline Ratings

DISCIPLINES THAT CREATE SUSTAINABLE VALUE	YOUR COMPANY RATING 1= WEAK 2= OK 3= STRONG	IMPORTANCE TO VALUE A=HIGHEST B=HIGH C=MEDIUM D=LOW
1. STRATEGIC PLAN THAT IS COMPELLING TO YOU, OWNERS, MANAGEMENT, AND THE TEAM		
2. OPERATING GOALS AND ACTIONS		
3. COMPENSATION TIED TO OPERATING GOALS		
4. KEY INDICATORS TRACKED MONTHLY OVER TIME		
5. COMPETENT, RESPECTED, SUPPORTED CEO		
6. SUCCESSION AND MANAGEMENT DEVELOPMENT		
7. FINANCIAL INFORMATION IS TIMELY, ACCURATE, AND UNDERSTANDABLE: P&L AND BALANCE SHEET		
8. MANAGEMENT INFORMATION THAT IS TIMELY, ACCURATE, AND CLEAR		
9. AUDITED FINANCIALS AND TRANSPARENCY		
10. SHAREHOLDER ALIGNMENT ON KEY ISSUES AND DIVIDENDS		
11. COMMUNICATIONS UP AND DOWN THAT ARE OPEN, HONEST, FREQUENT, AND MEANINGFUL		
12. FAIRNESS AND ETHICS STANDARDS ARE HIGH		
13. EMPLOYEES WHO ARE ENGAGED, COMPETENT, AND HAPPY		
14. PROCESSES TO REVIEW STATE OF THE COMPANY AND PROGRESS-ACCOUNTABILITY		
15. RISK LEVEL IS NORMAL (DEBT, CUSTOMER CONCENTRATION, ETC.)		
16. DISCIPLINED DECISION MAKING		
17. BOARD FUNCTION IS EFFECTIVE AND EFFICIENT		
18. OWNERS ARE HAPPY AND GETTING WHAT THEY WANT		
TOTAL		

IF TOTAL IS FORTY-FIVE OR HIGHER, COMPANY PROCESSES ARE PROBABLY READY FOR A STRONG ENDGAME.

IF TOTAL IS THIRTY TO FORTY-FIVE, THE COMPANY NEEDS A YEAR BEFORE IT CAN ACHIEVE A STRONG ENDGAME.

IF TOTAL IS LESS THAN THIRTY, THE COMPANY NEEDS TWO TO THREE YEARS AND MANAGEMENT CHANGES BEFORE IT CAN ACHIEVE A STRONG ENDGAME.

Appendix B
Advisory Board Charter

I. Advisory Board Mission:

The Advisory Board was formed to provide consulting and coaching to the CEO and management team in their quest to grow the business and build sustainable value.

This Advisory Board was formed and is convened at the discretion of ownership. This body of advisors can only provide suggestions about aspects of the business and cannot direct, bind, or obligate the corporation in any manner and is not to be construed as a de facto Board of Directors.

II. Formation

The Advisory Board size will be between three and six members.

Membership Composition. These characteristics include but are not limited to the following:

1. *No conflicts of interest, current or potential—a truly independent "outsider."*

2. *A successful professional who will have the respect of the management team, customers, vendors, and the financial community.*

3. *An individual who will be active and can contribute.*

4. *One who has a broad, practical business experience coupled with lots of common sense.*

5. *A decision maker, most likely an experienced CEO or COO.*

6. *Someone who will balance or counterbalance the experience, background, and circle of influence of the other Advisors.*

7. Someone who can be compatible with other Advisors and help create a working team, yet willing to make independent suggestions that he or she feels will help the companies reach their stated goals.

8. Someone who has the insight and perception to ask penetrating questions, but the discretion to make constructive suggestions.

9. Someone familiar with and who understands financial statements.

III. Expectations:

Board of Advisors

1. Be prepared for every meeting.

2. Review monthly financial package and contact Stakeholders as deemed appropriate.

3. Be available for consultation between board meetings.

4. Be respectful of meeting schedules and everyone's time.

5. Cooperate and support the Meeting Chairman and Facilitator.

6. Provide constructive criticism.

7. Hold stakeholders and management accountable for "suggested" action initiatives.

8. Provide introductions to vendors, financial resource, new team members, and other beneficial contacts.

9. Acknowledge progress and "wins."

Management

❖ Build and maintain financial discipline.

❖ Communicate with openness and honesty.

❖ Show a sense of urgency and respect for suggestions or "action initiatives."

❖ *Don't be defensive—listen carefully.*

❖ *Stay out of the operational "soup."*

IV. Member Performance Review:

The CEO will make a yearly informal review of each Member's continuation on the Advisory Board and will communicate any desired change in board members.

V. Committees:

At the discretion and direction of the CEO, Financial Review, and Salary Review committees may be formed to assist management.

VI. Compensation:

1. Meeting fees will be _____ per meeting. This fee will be reviewed yearly.

2. A retainer may be paid.

3. Consulting by individual Advisory Board members will be paid on an hourly basis as negotiated by the CEO and board member.

4. Expenses incurred for sanctioned meetings will be reimbursed by the company.

5. Advisory Board members will be part of a "value participation program" as developed by the company that allows Advisory Board members to share in the gain created during the board members' tenure on the Board of Advisors.

VII.   Confidentiality:

The oral and written content of all board or committee meetings shall be held in strict confidence.

All board members are required to sign a Non-Disclosure Agreement.

VIII.   Solicitation and Unfair Competition:

During his or her term of service and for a period of one year thereafter, an Advisory Board member may not solicit an employee, whether management or otherwise, for employment in a business enterprise directly or indirectly owned, managed, or directed by the board member. At all times during his or her service, the Advisory Board member may carry on any other business enterprise he or she owns or manages; however, it is understood that direct or indirect competition with the corporation shall be considered unfair competition during the board member's term. Prior to service, the board member shall either withdraw from such business activities or voluntarily resign from or not begin service upon the board. Each board member shall disclose, in confidence, solely to the Chief Executive Officer, his or her possibly competing business enterprises before commencing service on the board.

XI. Letter of Indemnification:

All Advisory Board members will receive a letter of indemnification from the company and be added to the Company's D&O Insurance Policy.

Appendix C
Strategic Planning Questions

1. **What are the three most significant issues you need to address as you look three years ahead?**

2. **What changes do you feel are possible in the following areas over the next three years?**

	Now	Three Years from Now
Sales		
Customers		
Products		
Services		
Facilities		
Systems		
People		
Profits		
Processes		
Competitors		
Government		
Legal		
Other		

3. **What are our greatest strengths? (List three to five)**

4. **What are our significant weaknesses? (List three to five)**

5. **What are our biggest opportunities? (List three to five)**

6. **What are the threats to our future?**

7. **What are the implications of technological changes on our operations and our connection with our present and future customers?**

8. **What do the owners expect from this company over the next three years? What are their concerns?**

9. **If you had an extra $1,000,000 to invest in this business, what investment would add the most value to this company?**

10. **What needs to get done in the next one hundred days to launch this company to the next level of strength and value?**

11. **What are the three actions you will take in the next one hundred days to move your company toward its Vision?**

Appendix D

Key Performance Indicator Examples,
Pet Food Company

Pipeline Measures:	Actual	Target
Customer Service Level		
Unit fill %	86.90%	92.00%
Order fill %	TBD	TBD
Sales Forecast Accuracy %	36.60%	85.00%

People Measures:		
Hourly Head Count	96	98
Hourly Head-count Costs	172.5	179.1
Hourly OT Hours	1016.8	488
Hourly OT Costs	15	9.5
Salaried Head Count	21	22
Salaried Head-Count Costs	183	186
Temporary Head Count	105	105
Temporary Head Count Costs	79.1	80.6
Lost Time Accidents	0	

Sales Analysis:		
Cat Food Sales	826	871
Dog Food Sales	6,591	5,828
Total Sales	7,417.60	6,699

P&L Measures:		
Gross Profit %	44.80%	43.10%
Operating Profit %	20.70%	17.60%
EBITDA %	13.80%	18.20%

Balance Sheet:

Days Accounts Receivable	59.3	61.86
Days Accounts Payable	37.7	36.55
Days Inventory	67.8	82.28
Total Liabilities to Equity	0.4	0.5
Company Value*	$58,500	$75,000

*6 times rolling 12 months of EBITDA

Appendix E
The Chairman's Playbook Checklist

Playbook Section	Item	Needed by	Status
Board Process and Structure			
1	Board Charter	B	
2	Board Calendar	B	
3	Board Composition	A	
4	Committees	C	
5	Meeting Agenda	A	
6	Chairman's Duties	B	
7	CEO's Rules of Engagement	B	
Company Organizational Documents			
8	Code of Ethics	C	
9	Corporate Governance Communication	B	
10	Disaster/Crisis Plan	C	
11	Compensation Plan	B	
12	Organization Plan	B	
13	Safety Plan	C	
Legal Instruments			
14	Buy/Sell Agreement	A	
15	Corporate Bylaws	A	
16	D&O Insurance	A	
17	Indemnification Agreement	A	

18	Non-Compete Agreement	A	
19	Intellectual Property Agreement	A	
20	Non-Disclosure Agreement	A	
21	Shareholder Agreement	A	
Management Preparation			
22	Annual Operating Plan	B	
23	Annual Financial Plan	A	
24	Auditor's Management Letter	C	
25	Capital Expenditure Budget	C	
26	Credit Agreement	B	
27	Financial Contingency Plan	C	
28	Key Indicators and Dashboard	B	
29	Strategic Plan	B	
30	90-Day Plan	B	
31	Vision-Future State	B	

Importance: A = Required by First Board meeting, B = Ready for Second Board meeting,   C = Ready beginning of Fiscal Year

Appendix F
Family-Owned Business Resources

1. **National Association of Corporate Directors**—NACD's mission is to advance exemplary board leadership—for directors, by directors. www.nacdonline.org

2. **Family Business Institute,** Harvard Business School leverages the strengths of family business management and successfully implements practices that drive high performance, shareholder loyalty, and healthy family relationships. www.exed.hbs.edu/programs/fib

3. **Family Firm Institute** is the leading membership association worldwide for professionals serving the family enterprise field. www.ffi.org

4. **Glenn Ayres & Associates** consults to family businesses facing challenges of ownership, governance, succession, leadership, management development, and conflict resolution. www.gayresandassociates.com

5. **Aspen Family Business Group** is a resource to families in business and provides professional services, conferences, and individual coaching. www.aspenfamilybusiness.com

6. **The Board Group,** founded by the authors of this book, is dedicated to helping owners of family-owned businesses create sustainable value through effective board work. www.theboardgroup.com

Appendix G
Outline for Selecting an Investment Banker

SKILL SETS

1. Knowledge of your industry and connections within

2. Communication skills, especially with numbers

3. Natural strategic thinking: Where does your business fit? What is the best structure?

4. Problem solver: When issues arise, will solutions be creative?

5. Knowledge of tax, legal, and accounting issues likely to arise

6. Experience in deals of your size and internally structured to support this size

7. Negotiating strength and command: During presentations, what role will they play? Are they a great opening act for your presentation?

ENGAGEMENT TERMS: ACTIVITIES

1. Due diligence of your company

2. Preparation of teaser

3. Preparation of Offering Book

4. Presentation of information to appropriate audience

5. Negotiation of deal

6. Documentation

7. Closing

DEAL SUPPORT AND COSTS

1. Limited period of time, broken down according to task

2. Fee based on sale proceeds with structured schedules

3. Fees related to earn outs and installment sales

4. Moneys required up front and back end

5. Guaranteed minimum fees to investment advisors

6. Expense reimbursement and limits

7. Exclusivity and carve outs

8. Availability of personnel most critical to you

9. Hourly charges for specialized assistance

About The Board Group

The Board Group comprises a group of experienced CEOs and board members who have broad experience with middle-market, privately-held, and public companies. In addition to serving on boards as chairman and board members, they help owners and CEOs find other board members that bring the right skills and experience to fit the needs of the companies they serve. The authors, John Zaepfel and Bill Hawfield, founded this organization.

How to Reach Us

The Board Group
3075 E. Thousand Oaks Blvd
Westlake Village, CA 91362
www.theboardgroup.com
gamechanging@theboardgroup.com
www.gamechangingadvisoryboards.com
805-497-3040

Index

Made in the USA
Charleston, SC
20 February 2016